Italy beyond Gomorrah

Disruptions

Disruptions is a series that interrogates and analyses disruptions within and across such fields and disciplines as culture and society, media and technology, literature and philosophy, aesthetics and politics.

Bearing Society in Mind: Theories and Politics of the Social Formation, Samuel A. Chambers
Open Education: A Study in Disruption, Pauline van Mourik Broekman, Gary Hall, Ted Byfield, Shaun Hides and Simon Worthington
What Lies Between: Void Aesthetics and Postwar Politics, Matt Tierney
Martial Arts Studies, Paul Bowman
Living Screens: Reading Melodrama in Contemporary Film and Television, Monique Rooney
Word: Beyond Language, Beyond Image, Mariam Motamedi Fraser
Culture and Eurocentrism, Qadri M. Ismail
Against Value in the Arts and Education, edited by Sam Ladkin, Robert McKay and Emile Bojesen
Imprints of Revolution: Visual Representations of Resistance, Guadalupe García and Lisa B. Y. Calvente
Disrupting Maize: Food, Biotechnology and Nationalism in Contemporary Mexico, Gabriela Méndez Cota
Transitioning: Matter, Gender, Thought, E. J. Gonzalez-Polledo
Italy beyond Gomorrah: Roberto Saviano and Transmedia Disruption, Floriana Bernardi

Italy beyond Gomorrah

Roberto Saviano and Transmedia Disruption

Floriana Bernardi

ROWMAN &
LITTLEFIELD
INTERNATIONAL
London • New York

Published by Rowman & Littlefield International Ltd
Unit A, Whitacre Mews, 26–34 Stannary Street, London SE11 4AB
www.rowmaninternational.com

Rowman & Littlefield International Ltd. is an affiliate of Rowman & Littlefield
4501 Forbes Boulevard, Suite 200, Lanham, Maryland 20706, USA
With additional offices in Boulder, New York, Toronto (Canada), and Plymouth (UK)
www.rowman.com

British Library Cataloguing in Publication Data
A catalogue record for this book is available from the British Library

ISBN: HB 978-1-78660-017-2
PB 978-1-78660-018-9

Library of Congress Cataloging-in-Publication Data Available

ISBN: 978-1-78660-017-2 (cloth : alk. paper)
ISBN: 978-1-78660-018-9 (pbk. : alk. paper)
ISBN: 978-1-78660-019-6 (electronic)

∞™ The paper used in this publication meets the minimum requirements of American National Standard for Information Sciences – Permanence of Paper for Printed Library Materials, ANSI/NISO Z39.48–1992.

Printed in the United States of America

Contents

Acknowledgements

First and foremost, my utmost gratitude for the opportunity to publish this book goes to Paul Bowman, the Disruption Series Editor at Rowman & Littlefield International, who considered my work worthy to be addressed to an international audience. For me, he has always been an example of extreme professionalism and cordiality, encouraging my projects with respect and enthusiasm. I really owe a lot to him, including the possibility to collaborate with the School of Journalism, Media and Cultural Studies at Cardiff University (UK) as a visiting researcher associate in year 2015/2016. Of course, this publication would not have been possible were it not for the other people who showed appreciation for this editorial project and worked variously on this book: the editorial assistants, Martina O'Sullivan first and Michael Watson later, the advisory board members and the anonymous and non-anonymous readers who reviewed the book proposal and the finished volume. Each of them gave me precious advice and confidence. I would also like to express my deepest gratitude to Patrizia Calefato, who guided and supported early research for this work during my PhD years at the University of Bari Aldo Moro (Italy), and to all the colleagues and friends who shared ideas, impressions, suggestions and still-unpublished documents with me. Particularly, I owe my thanks to Roberto Derobertis, Alessandro Pecoraro, Chiara Faggiolani, Valeria Castelli, and to the organizers and participants to the challenging conferences and seminars where some of the issues discussed in this book were first presented: the 'Transforming Audiences Conference 2' at London Westminster University (UK) in September 2009, the 'Italian Cultural Studies Conference' at Dartmouth College (USA) in May 2010 and the seminars on the sixty years of Rai Television at the University of Bari (Italy) in December 2014. Furthermore, a special note of thanks also goes to Roberto Saviano for inspiring this research with his great civil passion, although I cannot hide a certain amount of disappointment for having left unaccomplished the agreed project of an interview for this book.

Finally, this book is dedicated to my family, mum and dad, my beloved Nick and our soon-to-be-born baby Alberto.

ONE

Introduction

Italy beyond *Gomorrah*

POSITIONINGS #1: THE OBSERVER

Edgar Morin maintained that whatever the phenomenon approached by a scholar is, it is also necessary that the scholar himself or herself becomes the object of study, since his or her figure could disturb the study object or, to some extent, he or she could project himself or herself in it. According to Morin, whatever research one starts in the field of humanities, the first steps to accomplish are self-analysis and self-criticism (Morin 1962: 16). Accordingly, I would like to start this book clarifying my positioning towards the subject-object of study: Roberto Saviano as a public persona and the media, cultural and political phenomenon engendered by the publication of his non-fiction novel *Gomorra. Viaggio nell'impero economico e nel sogno di dominio della camorra* in 2006 (hence referred to as *Gomorrah*, if not differently specified).

When *Gomorrah* came out, I read it in one breath, as I was fascinated by its pressing, passionate and outraged writing style, a writing of resistance and vision alike. This reading was an 'event' (Bowman 2011: 116); it definitely marked a transformative moment in my perception of reality, both of the reality immediately next to me and of the much more distant reality, yet rooted in the same flows of criminal ideology and money. After my 'encounter' with *Gomorrah* something 'happened': the urgency to know and understand these power dynamics, hidden to general public and to the majority of citizens until then, became pressing for me. Also, it provoked even greater awareness and certainty about the value of people's knowledge and responsibility in individual actions within a community, especially in common everyday life choices. Indeed, *Gomorrah* changed my way of thinking and disrupted my 'language', if we mean by this term the 'Umwelt', that is the modelling social practice by means of which individuals mould themselves, organize and plan the world around them, producing signs and values within different social contexts and human relationships among people (Calefato 2008).

Then, in the following years, I have eagerly followed Roberto Saviano's voice, finding it always convincing and trustworthy; I have read every new article, and I have watched and listened to every TV, radio and web contribution of his. When possible, I have also been present at some of his public events: in a public square of Polignano a Mare in a hot and humid Apulian summer night; in the Feltrinelli library of Bari for the launch of the books *Vieni via con me* (2011b) and *Zero Zero Zero* (2013); at the 'Piccolo Teatro' of Milan in February 2010 and, finally, in April 2016 when I enthusiastically managed to have a conversation with the author in the theatre backstage after his performance.

During my waits before the entrance in theatres and libraries protected by the police, while I was standing in incredibly long queues together with dozens and dozens of my (almost) peers looking forward to exchanging a few words with the 'writer-pop star', receiving an autograph on their books or taking a picture with him, I perceived the absolute singularity of all those situations. That huge multitude of people was not crowding there for a popular musician, singer or famous actor, but for a young journalist and writer who usually deals with mafia issues, often reckoned as boring and difficult matters to understand for the vast majority of non-expert public. While I was talking to some of the people in the long queues, or 'stealing' some information from the crowd here and there, it was evident that those multitudes were mostly made up of 'fans' of Roberto Saviano. Almost all of them were Saviano's assiduous readers and spectators, and they were generally very 'attached' to that man/writer as they invested (or had invested) a high degree of emotions and affections in him. I could not stop wondering how and why this process had been possible: I wondered how it had been possible that an audience mostly numbed by the almost edulcorated journalistic and mainstream media narrations about Italy – a country in ruins from a political, social and economic point of view – always gathered in such copious quantity to listen to a fierce and yet visionary narration of reality, a narration based on people's responsibility and (counter) power, as single individuals and as a community. Did all this happen only thanks to the power of mainstream cultural industry, and particularly thanks to highly influential editorial and television marketing? Did all this happen thanks to the power of the 'author-brand' Roberto Saviano, whose logos are *Gomorrah* covers, the writer's name and face on newspapers, magazines and advertisings? Or rather, did this also happen for different reasons, involving values, passions and affections, which do not exclude, nevertheless, the risky and undecidable appeal of Roberto Saviano as a text, symbol and cool brand, at least so far? This was the starting point of my research.

Therefore, this book suggests a possible reading and deconstructive interpretation of the huge alterdisciplinary media event developed around Saviano after the publication of his best-seller *Gomorrah* (2006c). Particularly, it investigates the conditions and modalities by which this phenomenon started, the several disruptions Saviano provoked in Italy with his first book and subsequent transmedia interventions, and his cultural translation and reception into a mainly Anglo-American context. Additionally, by means of a focus on Saviano's disruptive work and the representation of his charismatic body redefining the figure and task of the modern intellectual, I will try to highlight both the agency of literature and the relevance of Internet and major social networks in the creation of networks of subjectivities. As I hope it will be clear, these are the latest useful tools to establish ethical-political duties grounded in a 'passional communication' between the writer and his audience as well as in a micropolitics of affects. Simultaneously, the book intends to provide a cross-sectional insight into Italy in the (post-)Berlusconi age through an understanding of Saviano's transmedia work.

POSITIONINGS #2: THE RENARRATION OF THE AUTHOR-BRAND

In the Anglo-American market

Before starting the deconstruction of the phenomenon Saviano with a principal focus on Italy, the country where it originated, in this short introduction I would like to give an account of the narrative frames allowing the construction of the literary fame of Roberto Saviano in the Anglo-American book market. According to Serena Bassi, in spite of the well-documented resistance to translation in the Anglo-American book markets (2015: 3), Roberto Saviano, an unknown and translated author, has been capable of reaching best-selling status even there. As Bassi puts it, this is due to the fact that 'the effectiveness with which a book is marketed may largely depend on the story that is being told about the book and its author' and its appeal to current tastes. Indeed, Bassi uses the notion of 'author-brand', a media-friendly and recognizable personality with which to sell the literary product, to explain the renarration of Roberto Saviano in Britain and the USA. Particularly, for Bassi 'an author-brand is often made up of a story of what the author is like as a person, how she or he came to write that particular book and what significance the publication of the book had in her or his life' (3). In the case of Roberto Saviano, Bassi argues that when he began to attract the attention of the British media, by the end of 2006, Saviano was first translated in accordance with the Italian articulation of his author-brand, that is a national anti-Mafia hero (see chapter 2). Later on, instead, when the news of a bomb attack intended to kill him before Christmas was out in 2008, followed by an open letter signed by six Nobel Prize winners in solidarity with the writer, the narrative frame for Saviano's 'author-brand' translation changed. Since then, both in the British and in the American press, the Italian writer has started to be associated with Indian author Salman Rushdie. Roberto Saviano became addressed as 'Italy's Salman Rushdie' – the author of *The Satanic Verses* (1988) condemned to death together with his publishers by a fatwa pronounced by Ayatollah Khomeini – and as 'a symbol of the universal right to freedom of speech'. Of course, as Bassi points out, the comparison between the writers was based on their biographies, not on their literary style or issues faced, and it served to foreground the fact that Saviano was forced into hiding following the publication of his book. Additionally, according to Bassi, this representation was coherent with the widespread narrative of a present marked by global threats and insecurity dominating media and Western state institutions in the aftermath of the September 11 attacks, including in Italy (Brunetti and Derobertis 2014). Finally, in Bassi's view, Saviano is part of the flourishing intellectual industry of 'the scenario trade', including journalists, academics, film directors and popular writers, defined as 'scenarists', who compete for promoting their specific 'scenario' to become the one that is most frequently referred to (11). Accordingly, as a 'scenarist', Saviano presents himself as capable of providing us with a map of the world we live in, based on the metanarrative of globalization and economic world order discussed in *Gomorrah*. Thanks to these strategies, the book marketing working for the cultural translation of author-brand Roberto Saviano in English has justified the reasons why Saviano deserved (and deserves) a translation in the Anglo-American market; that is, the critique of organized crime within the global capitalist economy Saviano has also discussed in *Zero Zero Zero* (2013), his second non-fiction novel dealing with drug trade, cocaine and world criminal capitalism.

As I wrote before, and as we are going to see throughout the book, the power of mainstream cultural industry, the highly influential editorial and television marketing and the power of the 'author-brand' are all crucial factors in our case study. Nevertheless, they are only *some* of its crucial factors. Indeed, from a semiotic perspective, insofar as 'Roberto Saviano' can be recognized as a brand, it/he suggests values towards which we should tend as well as individual senses and social meanings in the name of which it builds, articulates and enacts its subjective identity (Marrone 2007: 333). For, brands have always to do with narratives and passions, identity and communication, enunciations and plurality of voices, styles and genres; they have also to do with bodies and sensoriality, as well as with figurative and visual strategies. As it is evident, these are all semiotic phenomena constitutive of brands expressing their inner essence and truth (334). Brands are discursive constructions produced by a number of underlying processes of signification involving different aspects: economic, social and cultural (15); for this reason, most of the elements related to brands I have listed earlier will be discussed in the book. In other words, my focus is not 'Roberto Saviano' as a *brand* in itself, but on the complex network of processes of signification and relations constituting the *branding* of a new discursive formation for Italy.

POSITIONINGS #3: LOOKING BEYOND

The idea of 'beyond' lying underneath the title of this book is multifaceted. First, in its simplest deployment, the word refers to what happened in Italy after the publication of *Gomorrah* in terms of reactions to this book. Specifically, it refers to the literary and cultural debate the book aroused (chapters 2 and 3), Saviano's following transmedia interventions and disseminations (chapter 3) and people's massive demonstrations of solidarity with the writer after he was assigned police protection, which started within the virtual world or the so-called beyond measure realm (chapter 4).

Second, the term 'beyond' hints at the backlit representation of Italy emerging from my narration and analysis of the phenomenon Roberto Saviano. The returning image one can get highlights a largely widespread corruption, criminal organizations' infiltrations into economy, politics and communication, an eternally unsolved southern question, high unemployment rates, gender and class divide and also a great deal of conservatism in the cultural industry and in most intellectuals' approach to it. Thus, the picture seems to show a country stuck at an impasse, where the state of things always stays more or less the same and where, despite people's awareness and numerous surges of upheaval, the only possible solutions to this complex condition seem to be emigration or an eternal uneven fight of resistance.

However, third and more importantly, the word 'beyond' makes reference to a specific historical conjuncture of Italy, the period of and after the publication of *Gomorrah* (2006c), characterized by what I deem as a crisis. But let me explain it better. As Stuart Hall puts it, 'A conjuncture is a period during which the different social, political, economic and ideological contradictions that are at work in society come together to give it a specific and distinctive shape' (Hall and Massey 2010: 57). Additionally, with reference to Gramsci's thought, Hall uses the notion of conjuncture in a broader sense: 'As a way of marking significant transitions between different political moments; that is to say, to apply it as a general system of analysis to any historical situation' (58). Accordingly, still following Hall, in order to analyse a conjuncture it is necessary to describe how the complex power of hegemony works at its different levels of expression: political, ideological, common sense, cultural and economic (65). Nevertheless, conjunctures can be interrupted and disrupted; therefore the in-between space between two different conjunctures is usually characterized by a 'crisis', defined by Hall as the period when 'the contradictions that are always at play in any historical moment are condensed, or, as Althusser said, fuse in a ruptural unity'. In Hall's view, crises are 'moments of potential change' whose outcome is not given or predetermined; indeed, society may move on to another version of the same conjuncture, or to a somewhat transformed version of it, or relations can be radically transformed (57).

Well, when Saviano published *Gomorrah* (2006c), Italy was still living under a Berlusconian conjuncture which, however, was slowly coming to an end after dragging Italy to general decline, in coincidence with the no longer-hideable tragic wave of effects on the country caused by the collapse of the global financial and bank system Berlusconi had always tried to deny. From a Western and worldly perspective, the conjunctural crisis we are still going through started in the economy, and probably so it was in Italy too. However, as I wrote before, every conjunctural crisis is also a crisis of politics, culture, ideology, and sometimes it is exactly the task of intellectuals that of creating crisis. This is what Umberto Eco argues when, in dialogue with Stuart Hall advocating both an analytical task and an 'anticipatory function' of intellectuals, he affirms that nowadays perhaps the task of intellectuals is to meditate on how to help governments in solving the crisis and to show the way to turn upside down the sense of disillusionment and powerlessness every crisis carries with it (Eco and Hall 1985: 115).

This sense of disillusionment and powerlessness was largely felt in Italy when *Gomorrah* came out. Therefore, as I am going to show throughout the book, my claim is that Saviano's work did provoke a crisis in the country: his interventions caused disruptions in many realms of culture: literature, journalism, media, politics, in the way of perceiving Italy and the global market, in people's perception of mafia issues and also in the representation of intellectuals. The point now is to understand whether this crisis has actually led to a radical rupture of the previous paradigm or whether it has been just a temporary crisis where social forces have been unable to transform things very deeply, and which has been (or will be) basically followed by a return to a 'business as usual' condition.

Finally, the word 'beyond' is here to be meant as a period of transition, still open and undefined, where what we can do as scholars and citizens is reasoning on what has been left behind and what can be envisioned for the future, beyond the event of *Gomorrah*.

POSITIONINGS #4: READERSHIP

The book is addressed both to specialist audience interested in study fields like Italian contemporary literature and culture, cultural studies, sociology of culture and communication, media and journalism studies, social semiotics, political theory and activism, translation studies, and to non-specialist audience, simply interested in Roberto Saviano and his production and ethical-political intervention. For this reason, I have done my best to write a readable book both for academics and for non-specialist readership. However, expert readers will soon recognise the interdisciplinary approach to the subject matter, mainly oriented from a socio-semiotic perspective – meant as the whole of discourses and practices intervening in the formation and/or transformation of the conditions of interactions among individual and collective subjects (Marrone 2001: xvii) – but also integrated with a number of core notions of cultural, audience and translation studies.

To my knowledge, until now no volumes have been published dealing with a complete and detailed analysis of Roberto Saviano as a writer and media phenomenon. Therefore, another main objective of this book is to fill this empty space and provide a thorough and scientific analysis of Roberto Saviano's work, especially suitable for non-Italian readers. The readers will tell if my intention was a too ventured pretension, yet I hope this book will remain an honest account to an interesting page of Italian contemporary culture.

TWO

Who is Saviano?

Undecidability of an intellectual-pop star

DISRUPTIONS IN THE ITALIAN DEBATE ON INTELLECTUALS

With his article titled 'Intellettuali, non una voce – il declino dell'intellettuale italiano' (Intellectuals, not a single word – the decline of the Italian intellectual), published in the Italian newspaper *l'Unità* on 18 February 2004, literary critic Romano Luperini aroused a strong debate on the need of re-defining the task and function of contemporary intellectuals, a word which entered the Italian dictionary only under the Fascist regime. Luperini meant by *task* the duty assigned to intellectuals by institutions, implying knowledge and a whole of specific skills, in return for a wage; public or private funds for research; a status, some tasks – included the bureaucratic ones – and the collocation within a hierarchy. With the word 'function', instead, Luperini referred to the intellectual activity following its own logic, striving for freedom from conditionings, thus aiming at getting ahead of institutions and real authorities in order to obey just the ethics of research and the destinies of humankind. In the same article Luperini denounced the intellectual, political and economic decline of Italy, which had begun in the 1980s and which, in his opinion, had reached its peak in the first years of the new century. The reasons for this decline, emerging from the contributions to the debate of several writers and journalists, were to be found in the lack of cultural and political discussion among writers; the lack of dialog and controversy among critics and literary theorists; the impoverishment of Italian language due to the hegemony of political parties – particularly the ideology of Berlusconism; the media responsibility of reducing cultural complexity and producing icons to be sold, rather than writers able to influence the readers' world view.

This critique to mass media and cultural industry products as means of homologation actually dates back to the 1960s and 1970s in Italy (and mostly continues still today), coherently with a well-rooted tradition of scepticism and pessimism towards the new spirit of the postmodern time, which Theodor Adorno had theorized within the Frankfurt school. Despite some rare exceptions, such as Umberto Eco, who tried to subvert this line of thought in Italy with his book *Apocalittici e Integrati* (1964), and Adriano Olivetti, who chose to employ writers, poets and literary critics in the top positions of his prestigious typewriter company in the same years, Italian intellectuals have usually claimed a position of centrality in the public debate, without being willing to renounce their elitism and aristocratic detachment from the masses' cultural tastes, as well as to exploit the novelties and potential introduced by the cultural industry. This is certainly due both to the strong and long-lasting influence of Benedetto Croce's thought on Italian culture and to the so-called deficit model, namely the assumption of an inherent lack of cognition in subaltern classes (Antonello 2012: 58), at the basis of the relationship between cultural elites and the 'people-nation'.

In this climate of widespread conservatism, one of the last Italian intellectuals exerting a strong influence on the twentieth-century cultural debate was definitely Pier Paolo Pasolini (1922–1975), who led a struggle against the 'new consumeristic fascism', the 'cultural homologation' and the 'Italian anthropological mutation' from the front pages of *Corriere della Sera* between 1973 and 1975. Particularly, on 14 November 1974 Pasolini wrote an article, widely known as 'Io so' (I know), which was to be one of the last writings proving the public function of the intellectual, called to exert the duty of political intervention, especially in the most difficult periods in a country's history. May 2006, however, has come to be considered as a disruptive turning point in Italian literary landscape: it was the publication date of *Gomorra. Viaggio nell'impero economico e nel sogno di dominio della camorra*[1] is a book written by Roberto Saviano, a young writer-journalist born in Naples in 1979. With this book, a new *j'accuse*, a new denunciation – admittedly inspired by Pasolini – breaks the silence on Italian literature and livens up the reflection on its ability to 'write about the mechanisms of power', 'to pursue the dynamics of reality', 'without any metaphors or mediations except the blade of writing':

> I know and I can prove it. I know how economies originate and where their smell comes from. The smell of success and victory. I know what sweats of profit. I know. And the truth of the word takes no prisoners because it devours everything and turns everything into evidence. It doesn't need to drag in cross-checks or launch investigations. It observes, considers, looks, listens. It knows. It does not condemn to prison and the witnesses do not retract their statements. No one repents. I know and I can prove it. I know where the pages of the economy manuals vanish, their fractals mutating into materials, things, iron, time, and contracts. I know. The proofs are not concealed in some flash drive buried underground. I don't have compromising videos hidden in a garage in some inaccessible mountain village. Nor do I possess copies of secret services documents. The proofs are irrefutable because they are partial, recorded with my eyes, recounted with words, and tempered with emotions that have echoed off iron and wood. I see, hear, look, talk, and in this way I testify, an ugly word that can still be useful when it whispers, 'It's not true', in the ear of those who listen to the rhyming lullabies of power. The truth is partial; after all, if it could be reduced to an objective formula, it would be chemistry. I know and I can prove it. And so I tell. About these truths. (Saviano 2008e: 213)

On the relevance of the body in the 'affaire Saviano' I will focus more thoroughly in due course. However, it is good to stress since now that, differently from other intellectuals, Saviano speaks only in the name of his violated body, which is for him the primary tool to achieve knowledge and get to the truth: a 'partial' but 'irrefutable' truth, gained through the senses, 'tempered with emotions' and 'recounted with words'. He does no longer speak in the name of a strictly political and ideological perspective but on the basis of an experience which is physical and biological at the same time, before being an intellectual one.

This fundamental shift in the complex intellectual task of testifying and denouncing the mechanisms of power was soon emphasized by Romano Luperini, the Italian literary critic who hailed the publication of *Gomorrah* as a literary event with delight. In his introductory speech at the opening of the University of Siena academic year 2006–2007, Luperini described the book as the result of a researcher's work. Luperini, indeed, did not define Saviano as a man of letters or an intellectual, but as a young researcher with a temporary contract and a wage received by a public corporation named Osservatorio sulla camorra e l'illegalità. Moreover, he defined *Gomorrah* as a strange book, a hybrid of a documentary and a novel, an autobiography and an essay, a hybrid of literature and sociology: 'It was as if flexibility had taken a shape and had become an *oeuvre*, a new literary genre' (Luperini 2007; my translation from Italian). Furthermore, according to the critic, Saviano embodied Edward Said's figure of the marginal intellectual who does no longer aim to occupy the centre of the scene, and does not take part in a battle of manifestos, ideas and poetics, but accepts his marginality as a natural condition.

Nevertheless, whoever is acquainted with, or more simply intrigued by, the figure of Roberto Saviano could easily judge inappropriate the feature of marginality with reference to his public persona. Indeed, on several occasions Saviano has declared to be willing of 'exploiting the media echo and of not obeying to the low profile which is usually assigned to a writer' because his obsession is that of 'trying to change the state of things by means of his words' (2009b). As a matter of fact, Roberto Saviano has been able to 'sfondare la scena', as we say in Italian, to *shoot to fame* and conquer successfully every media space for visibility, thus turning himself into a much-debated figure of intellectual: loved or hatred, raised to a myth or denigrated, overestimated or deplored. So, who is Roberto Saviano? Is he a victim of the process of 'journalistization' of intellectuals? Is he subjected to the logics of selling and audience success? Is he manipulated by marketing and rhetoric? Is he responsible for reducing cultural complexity to produce a kind of knowledge which is acceptable and telegenic? In other words, does Roberto Saviano accomplish just a *task*, or does he rather exert a *function*?

THE 'AFFAIRE SAVIANO'

In order to answer these questions with plausible responses, it might be necessary to clarify how the 'affaire Saviano' or 'the media phenomenon Saviano' aroused. This affaire developed some months after the publication of *Gomorrah* in May 2006 by Mondadori, a leading publishing house owned by Silvio Berlusconi's family. Until that date, Roberto Saviano had been a journalist with a master's degree in Philosophy who, besides being a member of Osservatorio sulla camorra e l'illegalità, had published his articles on several newspapers, magazines and literary journals, such as *Corriere del Mezzogiorno, il Manifesto, Pulp, Diario, Sud, Nuovi Argomenti, Lo Straniero* and especially on the literary blog *Nazione Indiana*. Saviano's several television appearances, *Gomorrah*'s numerous book launches in many little and big bookshops and the request for buying the translation rights by the USA and many European states decreed huge interest in Roberto Saviano's non-fiction novel, allowing him to start precious collaborations with *La Repubblica* and *L'Espresso*, two of the largest circulating Italian daily newspapers and weekly magazines. In the meantime, also cinema production houses considered *Gomorrah* as an appealing book to be transposed into a film, and Fandango won the rights to transpose Saviano's book into a successful movie directed by Matteo Garrone.

The turning point in Roberto Saviano's life and in the audience's perception of his work, however, took place on 23 September 2006 when he pronounced a speech in the crowded central square of Casal di Principe, the stronghold of *Casalesi*, a fierce camorra clan. On that occasion Saviano pronounced a speech directly addressing the bosses, whose representatives were standing in the square:

> Strangely, for such a long time this land has not been told about. . . . I protest when the name camorra is associated to a territory which suffers camorra. Francesco Schiavone, Michele Zagaria, Antonio Iovine[2], go away! You do not belong to this land! [to the bosses] Ward off them! Demand not to implore what has been given to you by right. Being informed on how the mechanisms of contracts works, understanding and being acquainted with them is the only way to defend yourself. Do not let anyone extort your land. This land is yours! [to the listeners]. (Saviano 2010c)[3]

Hence the challenge and provocation to the camorra bosses start with one of the most basic linguistic actions, and yet one of the most complex ones: the act of naming. Saviano, who had already denounced the names of the bosses in *Gomorrah*, strengthens the power of telling and revealing the names as he dares to pronounce them from the same territory where the bosses are deemed as unnameable for the position of supreme power they occupy, thus continuing to unmask the history and legends of his area. In Casal di Principe's square, declares Saviano,

> I wanted to state that I was not afraid, that I am not afraid, and I wanted to show that in some way it was possible to pronounce their damned names. I have grown up in an area where the bosses' names are never pronounced, not for fear but for respect. 'He is the one who commands here', 'all this area belongs to him'. . . . Why one cannot use the name? Because you mustn't pronounce it in vain. . . . I wanted that all this could end, even if only for an hour, ten minutes . . ., but that it could end. . . . It's easy to challenge a boss from Naples, Rome, Milan; it's less easy doing it from their fortresses. Words have another meaning there. (2010c)[4]

This strict denunciation stated using the apparently simple and obvious linguistic act of naming, actually engendered many consequences which have to do with what Roland Barthes called the 'power of exploration' of names, with the birth of an undecidable popular culture discourse and with the exploitation of a much-debated all-media strategy. But let's analyse all these effects one by one.

As semiologist Patrizia Calefato explains, there is always a narrative principle in a name, in the real world as in fiction, and it is exactly this narrative principle that keeps the name alive as a sign; moreover, there is always a myth the name anchors itself to, being it a foundational myth or a prosaic myth of contemporaneity (Calefato 2006: 11). When we talk about criminal bosses, we talk exactly about (false) prosaic myths of contemporaneity; men and women whose figures are wisely built as faded caricatures of the protagonists of criminal movies. As an example, consider the following description of the bodyguards of a female boss in *Gomorrah*:

> They followed her in a Smart, the little two-seater car all the camorra women own. . . . In our fantasies female bodyguards look like bodybuilders, every muscle bulging like a man's, bunching thighs, pectorals swallowing breasts, overgrown biceps, necks like tree trunks. But there was nothing of the Amazon in the bodyguards I saw. One was short, with a big, flabby ass and hair dyed to look black; the other was thin, frail, and bony-looking.

> I was struck by the fact that both were wearing fluorescent yellow, the same colour as the Smart. The driver had on yellow sunglasses and the other a bright yellow T-shirt. A yellow that could not have been chosen by chance, a combination that could not have been a mere coincidence. A professional touch. The same yellow as Uma Thurman's motorcycle outfit in *Kill Bill*, the Quentin Tarantino film in which for the first time women are first-rate criminal stars. The same yellow that Uma Thurman wears in the ad for the film. . . . A yellow so unreal it becomes a symbol. (Saviano 2008e: 145)

When Roberto Saviano chose to mention the bosses' names in that square – more or less aware of the consequences this act would have meant to him (first and foremost the loss of his freedom) – he probably trusted the power of exploration that the use of proper names assures, according to Roland Barthes. For Calefato, when one mentions a name, one exerts a power; this means that a relationship is built between the person who speaks and the person who is named (Calefato 2006: 8). The most frequent words in Saviano's idiolect include the verb 'to tell' (*raccontare*) and the noun 'story' (*racconto*); therefore, before the unnameable and insolent power of criminality, Saviano considered the power of exploration of those names subjecting them to the power of counter-narration, namely the possibility of building new landscapes of resistance as well as civil and political agency, by means of the language of *denuncia*.

Nevertheless, the act of naming the bosses has damaged Saviano both as a citizen and as an intellectual. As a matter of fact, he was assigned police protection a month after that day in September, and from that moment on all his public interventions have been considered as the interventions of a symbol, the new icon of the fight against camorra and criminality in the decaying Italy of the new century, rather than the interventions of an intellectual. In an interview with Enzo Biagi, Saviano declared he was aware of the change in the perception of his figure in collective imagination after that linguistic act of *denuncia* which earned him the support of many Nobel Prize winners and young writers, politicians and thousands of citizens with several initiatives:

> I believe I have turned into a symbol. Challenging the bosses in the square of their real strongholds' territories does not actually imply a risk, but it opens up a possibility of emulation: if there's

> one who can do it, everyone could do the same. This was exactly what I wanted to do: I wanted to prove to young people, in that case Casal di Principe's young people, that Casalesi's clan had oppressed their land, [. . . and] was forcing them to live in conditions and situations that a human being does not deserve. Thus, challenging them, in a sense I have turned into a symbol. (Saviano 2007)[5]

THE CRITIQUES TO THE INTELLECTUAL-POP STAR

As a consequence, on the one hand Roberto Saviano was becoming an adulated symbol, but meanwhile, on the other hand, he was starting to be fiercely criticized. The person who attacked for the first time the linguistic and narrative structure of *Gomorrah*, as well as the ideas expressed in that book and its author, with a biting and jeering criticism, was Alessandro Dal Lago, a well-known Italian sociologist. According to Dal Lago, the affaire Saviano and the media phenomenon revolving around him is based on a misunderstanding:

> The transformation of an essentially media event into a morality play where what clashes are not points of view or analytical categories, but allegories, embodied symbols: firstly the Hero against the Crime (with variations like the Saint against the Evil or the Martyr against the Persecutors). (Dal Lago 2010: 20–21)[6]

Dal Lago mainly criticized *Gomorrah* and its author because, according to him, the 'phenomenon Gomorrah' was totally fit to the cultural spirit of contemporary Italy; thus it was not adequate to the impelling need to dismantle the ideology of Berlusconism. According to Dal Lago, indeed,

> in a country where the spread of knowledge is largely assigned to media and where conflicts are reduced to stereotypes, it is totally coherent that the one who leads the moral opposition against the organized crime is a writer-hero. When Saviano says that his mission . . . is that of starting a trend[7], he simply admits that he wants to promote a unanimous egalitarianism: Mondadori has published his book, most of newspapers sponsor it and everyone is happy. Right-wing, moderate and left-wing readers, after

> reading *Gomorrah*, will be convinced that they have contributed to the struggle against the organized crime, and they will be able to sleep peacefully and go back to their occupations. However, as it is known, trends start and finish. (2010: 21)[8]

Moreover, according to Dal Lago, Saviano tends to split the world into an obsessive binary scheme and his rhetoric of heroism, which in Italy is more marked than everywhere else and exerts an anaesthetic and diverting function. For Dal Lago, 'By relishing in the exceptional nature of behaviours or in supreme sacrifices, the public opinion conceals or forgets connivance, collusions, opportunism, omissions, double crosses' (81–82). For Dal Lago, *Gomorrah* and Saviano's popularity are neither due to Saviano's good skills as a writer, nor to the originality of the work and not even to the direct, intimate, empathetic relationship between the author and his readers (as Saviano always highlights, instead). Rather, it is due to a powerful stroke of luck followed by excellent marketing strategies carried out by Mondadori publishing house. Dal Lago believes that the birth of the media phenomenon Saviano has been possible because of the ideology of Berlusconism exalting the market and promoting a liberal editorial policy with a mercantile nature. However, according to him, if a writer claims to be the voice of truth in the realm of media (which abolishes, for its very nature, any possibility of authentic voices), then he or she enters the world of self-deceit (122–123).

Further criticism to Saviano has come from Silvio Berlusconi and Luigi De Magistris (Naples mayor and former magistrate, respectively), to name just the most relevant names belonging to two different political and cultural factions, as well as from a part of the public opinion. These attacks blame Saviano for making money out of Naples, damaging the image of the city and of Italy, exploiting Naples and its suburbs as the stage for movies and a TV series about camorra, emphasizing only the negative aspects of the city. Another interesting critique, instead, arrives from Alessandro Trocino, a journalist for Italian newspaper *Corriere della Sera*. Trocino (2011) includes the Neapolitan writer among the so-called pop stars of culture. Particularly, he denounces the modality and reasons leading these pop stars to success and the paradigm they have created or endorsed. The features Italian intellectuals and public personas like Giovanni Allevi, Andrea Camilleri, Beppe

Grillo and Carlo Petrini share, according to Trocino, are the inclination to conformism, the propensity towards emotionality and sentimentalism, the predilection for indignation for its sake, the inclination to simplification, the profusion of apocalyptic rhetoric, to quote just a few. For Trocino, all these traits are associated to the widespread mediatization of the pop stars of culture, their extreme vanity and populism. For this, Trocino maintains that the pop stars of culture are:

> the mirror of a country affected by a sentimental rhetoric, a fake-revolutionary maximalistic anti-illuminist country. . . . A country that buys Saviano's fetish-book to struggle against camorra and then snorts camorra cocaine in the toilets of Milan's Hollywood night club. . . . A *midcult* country trusting the miracles of mass self-education; the country which transforms the engagé writer into a bookshelf icon. . . . A country which prefers feeding itself with a permanent state of indignation, rather than actually trying to change the state of things. (Trocino 2011: 13–15, my translation from Italian)

THE CHARISMATIC BODY OF A TRANSMEDIA INTELLECTUAL

The shared feature of the aforementioned judgements, namely the scepticism against 'an essentially media event' imbued with Berlusconian ideology and, therefore, addressed to mass audience, actually reveals the traditional Italian hiatus between cultural industry and the so-called *high culture*. As I said before, leaving aside a few exceptions, Italian intellectuals usually despise any kind of popular product and, as a consequence, they are often unable to bridge the gap between 'art' and 'mass production', as well as to create 'genres of quality average products' (Morcellini and De Nardis 1998: 18; my translation from Italian).

What all the critiques listed earlier do not take into account, however, is a more accurate and in-depth analysis of the agency and power of popular texts, as well as of the uses people can do with the products and commodities of cultural industry, especially when they enter a net-like organization. And the net-like organization is a really crucial element in the affaire Saviano, as I am going to show throughout this book. As Foucault stated,

> Power is employed and exercised through a net-like organization. . . . In fact, it is already one of the prime effects of power that certain bodies, certain gestures, certain discourses, certain desires come to be identified and constituted as individuals. . . . The individual is an effect of power, and at the same time, or precisely to the extent to which it is that effect, it is the element of its articulation. (Foucault 1980, quoted by Bowman 2012: 47)

For his ability to make a myth of himself, engender clear audience's factions, as well as controversial discourses around his public persona, Roberto Saviano can definitely be considered as a pop culture phenomenon. His success is due both to his writings and to his transmedia personality, able to penetrate all media – newspapers and television, radio and social networks, cinema and theatre in the belief that media, if used without cynicism and cunning, are exactly what they mean: means allowing to break indifference and speak up aloud (Saviano 2009c; 2009d).

Born within the realm of mass culture, the media phenomenon Saviano, as every pop culture phenomenon, has permeated and meanwhile been permeated by national culture and ideology, building a 'corpus of symbols, myths and images concerning the practical and imaginary life, a system of projections and specific identifications' (Morin 1962: 12; my translation from Italian). In the following paragraphs I am going to show the reasons why, in my view, Saviano – a young journalist-writer – has become a 'celebrity' and a 'pop star of culture' and the relevance this transformation may have in the ideology of Italian culture.

As it happens to any star or celebrity, the cultural industry – and particularly in this case the book industry, which from the 1980s onwards has been incorporated into a larger multimedia corporate conglomerate integrating the literary production into the entertainment industry (Bassi 2015: 2) – has produced the iconic figure of Roberto Saviano and has developed specific marketing and advertising strategies to make this commodity as much profitable as possible. It is evident this goal has been reached. Like any star, Saviano seems to be naturally charismatic and loved by (TV) cameras; he seems to be fascinating for many people and, at the same time, absolutely intolerable by many others. Differently from celebrities, however, Saviano's life is not glamorous at all – because of the police protection – or maybe it is, if we mean by glamour the charm of his meetings with some of the greatest intellectuals in the world, and the acclamation of his audience always waiting for him in a queue for hours to attend his public interventions.

A scene crowds in around Roberto Saviano, if we mean by 'scene' what Claudia Attimonelli defines as the temporary and dynamic agglutination and interest of single individuals as swarms around a corpus of signs in movement. In Attimonelli's opinion, practices and languages converge towards this corpus of signs in movement which becomes recognizable because – and when – it recognizes itself as a corpus of heterogeneous material made up of objects – like clothes, accessories, instruments – *quasi*-objects, such as film, music, books and poetics, clothing style, and non-objects, like poses, mimicry, attitudes and jargon (Attimonelli and Giannone 2011: 22–28).

Nevertheless, the question is: what is the corpus of objects, *quasi*-objects and non-objects in which the fans' scene crowding around Saviano recognizes itself every time his public interventions are planned, being they are live or are mediated by television screens? If we observe Saviano's audience and fans, we find out that they do not share neither objects nor non-objects, as the *scene* is made up of people of all ages (although especially people in their thirties), men and women with different education level (although mainly with a university education). Nevertheless, what these people have in common is an interest in books, particularly in those written and suggested by Saviano himself, and the desire of reflection on specific topics, such as the bravery of *denuncia*, the ethical-political engagement, the will to know about sly media mechanisms (for instance the so-called 'macchina del fango'), the hope for a change for Italy and the Italians, the will for future and the faith in the agency of literature. All these themes bring the crowd to gather in a scene and move towards the condition of attentive audience, first, and aware citizens, later.

On the basis of what I have argued so far, it may be relevant to wonder whether the phenomenon Saviano was determined just by a superstructure, or whether it is more appropriate to say that the cultural industry has exploited the deepest needs of the audience following the journalist-writer in a passionate way in a specific historical period. In other words, the question is: what is Saviano's function as a cultural sign? Is it right to say that he interrupted a historical and discursive formation which did not satisfy and no longer satisfies the public, made up of citizens? As Stuart Hall writes, 'The meaning of a cultural symbol is given in part by the social field into which it is incorporated, the practices with which it articulates and is made to resonate' (Hall 1994: 484). Thus if it is true, as Volosinov maintained, that 'each living ideological sign has two faces' and that 'this inner dialectic quality of the sign comes out fully in the open only in times of social crisis or revolutionary change' (Volosinov quoted by Hall 1994: 485), then what are the features that make the symbol Roberto Saviano so special and what critical factors does our age present?

In his famous work titled 'Stars', Richard Dyer makes reference to Max Weber's essay *On Charisma and Institution Building* (1968), where the German scholar theorized the concept of charisma with reference to political theory and discusses this issue within the realm of stardom. Weber defined charisma as 'a certain quality of an individual's personality, by virtue of which he is set apart from ordinary men and treated as endowed with supernatural, superhuman, or at least superficially exceptional power or qualities' (Weber quoted in Dyer 2007). In the same essay, quoting Edward A. Shils, Dyer states that 'the charismatic quality of an individual as perceived by others, or himself [*sic*] lies in what is thought to be his connection with . . . some very *central* figure of man's existence and the cosmos in which he lives. The centrality, coupled with intensity, makes it extraordinary' (Dyer 2007: 83). Finally, since Dyer maintains that charismatic appeal is effective especially when the social order is uncertain, unstable and ambiguous, and when the charismatic figure or group offers a value, order or stability to counterpoise this (83), it would not be wrong to point out that the 'heroic' or pop star appeal of Roberto Saviano depends on his embodiment of the values in crisis in Italian contemporary society. Some of these values are legality, ethical and political responsibility; hence, it is necessary to start a counter-hegemonic counter-narration taking the form of journalistic truth, resistance to power and a new process of people's empowerment.

The issues of truth and truthfulness are particularly relevant in Saviano's affaire as they involve the body of the writer. As Raffaello Palumbo Mosca explains, 'Saviano's attempt has been that of creating a discourse in a Foucauldian sense, namely changing the rules of the production of truth within a community, exploiting the transmedia nature of his witness'. In this way the body becomes extraordinarily relevant in this project, as it is a 'synonym of truthfulness'. Indeed, the body means 'the presence in the world of the author-narrator' and lets 'half-view the person behind the personality who establishes the possibility of a contact between the experience portrayed and the readers' one'. Saviano's body as a transmedia intellectual is thus *both* a means of knowledge and perception of the visible, *and* the warranty of the truthfulness of his narration, which will be credible until the author of the narration itself will remain credible (Palumbo Mosca 2009: 316–317; my translation from Italian).

The excessive repetition of Roberto Saviano's body image, which in the sometimes-de-realising effect of cultural industry's transmediality can see its value and originality demeaned, puts into question the possibility of an intervention of his text[9] into the real world. This intervention, in fact, 'plays . . . on a very fragile equilibrium, on the possibility of a dialog between the writer (intellectual) and the reader, based on a cold passion, which is the precise opposite of sentimentalism. A passionate, open, listening coldness' (319; my translation from Italian).

SAVIANO'S UNDECIDABILITY AND STRATEGIES OF ALTERDISCIPLINARITY

As discussed so far, the affaire Saviano presents itself as an exemplary popular text: involving issues and themes of cultural, political, economic and ideological interest, as well as literary appeal; of course, it is a text so rich as to produce meanings which need to be studied in their multiple interrelations. In the following paragraphs I am going to suggest an interpretation of the popular icon Roberto Saviano which, despite being always subject to *undecidability*, could better explain how I prefer reading the work of the Neapolitan journalist-writer, mainly in opposition with most of the critiques made to him. To do this I cannot but start from the deconstruction of the terms 'popular' and 'undecidability'.

In his essay titled *Notes on Deconstructing the Popular* (1994), Stuart Hall discusses the concept of popular suggesting different meanings of the term: (1) what masses of people listen, read, consume and seem to enjoy to the full – a notion associated with the manipulation and debasement of the culture of people, as well as with the notion of the people as 'purely passive' and constantly living in a condition of 'false consciousness' (446); 2) popular as a synonym of 'popular culture', characterized by authenticity, autonomy and independence from the relations of cultural power and domination exerted by capitalist cultural industries, the first agents of 'mass manipulation and deception'. As an alternative to the previous definitions, both quite limited and insidious, Stuart Hall also suggests a third way to approach the deconstruction of the popular – which I believe to be the most proper way to deconstruct the affaire Saviano – implying an interpretation of culture as a 'constant battlefield'. As Hall writes,

> I think there is a continuous and necessarily uneven and unequal struggle by the dominant culture, constantly to disorganize and reorganize popular culture, to enclose and confine its definitions and forms within a more inclusive range of dominant forms. There are points of resistance; there are also moments of supersession. This is the dialectic of cultural struggle. In our times, it goes on continuously, in the complex lines of resistance and acceptance, refusal and capitulation, which make the field of culture a sort of constant battlefield. A battlefield where no-once-for-all victories are obtained but where there are always strategic positions to be won and lost. . . . The structuring principle of 'the popular', in this sense, is the tensions and oppositions between what belongs to the central domain of elite or dominant cultures, and the culture of the periphery. (446–448)

Thus, also Roberto Saviano as a public persona and a cultural symbol develops within the realm of a continuous tension between popular culture and dominant culture. Saviano's meaning as a cultural sign expressing the defence of legality, ethical and political responsibility and resistance to all forms of power will depend on the continuous struggle between the capitalist hegemonic forces of cultural industries Saviano remains relentlessly linked to and the forces of popular culture, embodied by the people consuming his works, who are more or less aware of the dynamics of power those hegemonic forces exert. Finally, his meaning will depend on the strategies of media action – before the ethical, political and literary ones – that Saviano will choose in order to promote a signification of his text coherent with the reasons and context in which his 'character' was born as a text.

The ambiguity of signification of Saviano as a text leads to the other term requiring clarification: 'undecidability'. This term is clearly borrowed from Jacques Derrida's vocabulary and designates the condition of uncertainty characterizing every situation of extreme complexity, in which, nevertheless, one could be forced to take a decision or get to conclusions. In this case, the situation of extreme textual complexity is the intense semiotic play engendering several stratifications of meanings around Roberto Saviano's iconic figure and work. The need/will of taking a decision, instead, or the need/will to take a stand on the debate on the intellectual-pop star, derives from the same questions mentioned earlier: Who is Roberto Saviano? Is he a victim of the process of 'journalistization' of intellectuals? Is he subjected to the logics of selling and audience success? Is he manipulated by marketing and rhetoric? Is he responsible for reducing cultural complexity to produce a kind of knowledge which is acceptable and telegenic? And also, to quote Calefato (2009), does he have the features of a 'classic' and 'timeless' cultural sign, or is he subject to 'time', 'obsolescence' and semiotic usury connected to it?

In this complexity, a practice that could help is surely that of deconstruction, that kind of event de-structuring and de-composing every complex system, as the text Saviano is. The major concern of deconstruction is to analyse 'how we come to decisions, the processes that we follow when coming to decisions, working things out, and constructing knowledge'. This is fundamental because, as Paul Bowman maintains, 'we should care about how decisions are made and interpretations are reached because they relate directly to how differences are made. How things are interpreted can make all the difference in the world'. According to Bowman, this is particularly true for pop culture, whose realm is 'a complex matter of *articulation*: of texts, productions, interventions and utterances that can become connected with other so-called 'realms'. . . . There is no reason why even supposedly trivial texts and moments of popular culture might not become articulated to (connected to, entangled with) (m)any other elements of the human world of culture, politics, society, history and economy, in complex and consequential ways' (2008: 6).

As it happens with any popular text, the deconstruction of the text Saviano and the interpretation we assign to it can be ethically and politically relevant; thus the interpretation of the popular icon Roberto Saviano that I suggest here cannot but derive from the British cultural studies which, locating itself and operating 'beyond' or 'after deconstruction' (Hall 2001) and taking into account culture's constitutively political character, have the ethical-political intervention as their founding disciplinary imperative. Quoting Valentine, Bowman explains that the 'political action necessarily entails a cultural dimension'; moreover, 'because the referent of culture is by its nature limitless, the relation between culture and politics extends beyond the restricted domain of politics understood as the mechanics of a formal system so that culture entails a political dimension' (2011: 25).[10]

Within this network of mutual relationships between intellectual practices, political action, cultural and political dimension, one might ask what Roberto Saviano's ethical-political intervention consists of and what are the action strategies through which his intervention has been carried out or is being carried out. Given that the notion of 'intervention' is essential in cultural studies, and given that it refers to the 'worldly vocation' of cultural studies or to the 'will to connect' of critical and intellectual practices to make differences that count in the real world – to use Hall's words – one could say that Roberto Saviano's intervention has caused a disruption in the hegemonic media flow, provoking a difference and a crisis, maybe for the very first time in Italy. Differently from the typical highbrow approach to the culture of most Italian intellectuals, Roberto Saviano embodies the ideal of intellectual work promoted in the international arena both by Stuart Hall and by Edward Said.

For Hall, whose idea of intellectual work has its roots in Antonio Gramsci's idea of organic intellectual, an intellectual has to be

> at the very forefront of intellectual theoretical work because, as Gramsci says, it is the job of the organic intellectual to know more than the traditional intellectuals do: really know, not just pretend to know, not just to have the facility of knowledge, but to know deeply and profoundly. . . . If you are in the game of hegemony you have to be smarter than 'them'. Hence there are no theoretical limits from which cultural studies can turn back. But the second aspect is just as crucial: that the organic intellectual cannot absolve himself or herself from transmitting those ideas, that knowledge, through the intellectual function, to those who do not belong, professionally, in the intellectual class. And unless those two fronts are operating at the same time, or at least unless those two ambitions are part of the project of cultural studies, you can get enormous theoretical advance without any engagement at the level of the political project. (2001: 103)

Spreading ideas and knowledge not only to those who belong to his professional class and exerting his intellectual function, Roberto Saviano has managed to practice what Bowman calls 'alterdisciplinarity', namely to 'intervene into and to alter *other* disciplinary discourses and their productions (knowledges) not by critiquing them from afar but by intervening into the disciplinary spaces of their production and legitimation – that is: getting inside knowledge, undoing methodologies and arguing in the other's language for other conclusions' (2011: 67).[11] Roberto Saviano mainly works outside academic institutions and within the spaces of knowledge production such as literature, journalism and media. In this way he *intervenes in* those disciplinary areas and penetrates *their* knowledge concentrating on political, cultural, social and economic matters asking for an effective action and change. For Said, instead, intellectuals 'are individuals with a specific public role in society that cannot be reduced simply to being a faceless professional, a competent member of a class just going about her or his business'. For him it is essential that

> the intellectual is an individual endowed with a faculty for representing, embodying, articulating a message, a view, an attitude, philosophy or opinion to, as well as for, a public, in public. . . . So in the end, it is the intellectual as a representative figure that matters: someone who visibly represents a standpoint of some kind, and someone who makes articulate representations to his or her public despite all sorts of barriers. . . . Intellectuals are individuals with a vocation for the art of representing, whether that is talking, writing, teaching, appearing on television; and that vocation is important to the extent that it is publicly recognisable and involves both commitment and risk, boldness and vulnerability. (Said 1993)

Said maintains that in the large amount of research carried out on the figure of intellectuals, too much space and time has been devoted to a definition of their task(s) and function, while too little space has been devoted to their image, signature, actual intervention and results, which all together represent the nourishment of every real intellectual. To avoid this risk, the core of the following chapters will be the analysis of Roberto Saviano's work mainly narrated in terms of his 'signature', disseminations and effects.

NOTES

1. If not differently specified, from now on I will use the abbreviation '*Gomorrah*' to refer to Roberto Saviano's book.

2. Francesco Schiavone, known as Sandokan, is the legendary moral boss of *Casalesi*, condemned to life imprisonment in June 2008. Antonio Iovine, instead,

condemned but fugitive at the moment of this speech, was arrested on 17 November 2010, while Michele Zagaria was arrested on 7 December 2011.

3. Italian original version: 'Per troppo tempo questa terra, stranamente, non è stata raccontata. . . . Io protesto quando viene associato il termine camorra a un territorio che subisce la camorra. Francesco Schiavone, Michele Zagaria, Antonio Iovine, andatevene! Non siete di questa terra, smettete di essere di questa terra. Respingiamoli! Non siete nessuno! Pretendete di non implorare quello che vi è stato dato per diritto. Guardare in faccia e sapere che conoscere come funziona il meccanismo degli appalti, conoscere . . . e capire è l'unico modo per difendervi. E soprattutto, non fatevi strappare la vostra terra da nessuno. Questa terra è vostra!'

4. Italian original version: 'volevo dire che non avevo paura, che non ho paura, e volevo dimostrare in qualche modo che era possibile fare i loro dannatissimi nomi. Io sono cresciuto in un territorio in cui i nomi dei boss non si pronunciano mai, non per paura ma per rispetto. 'Qua comanda lui', 'Questa è tutta zona di quello', 'Lì c'è chi sappiamo noi', 'lì c'è l'amico', 'lì c'è lo zio'. Perché non usare il nome? Perché non devi pronunciarlo invano. . . . Io volevo che questa storia finisse, anche soltanto per un'ora, dieci minuti, mezz'ora, ma finisse. . . . È facile attaccare un boss a Napoli, a Roma, a Milano, meno facile nei loro fortini. Lì la parola ha un altro significato' (ibid.).

5. Italian original version: 'Credo di essere diventato un simbolo, nel senso che sfidare in piazza i boss in territori considerati vere e proprie roccaforti, non ha un significato in sé di pericolo, ma lancia una gemma di possibilità di emulazione: se lo fa uno, lo possono fare tutti. Era esattamente quello che volevo fare: mostrare ai giovani, in quel caso di Casal di Principe, che il clan dei casalesi aveva schiacciato la loro terra, e non soltanto la loro terra, che li costringeva a vivere in condizioni, in situazioni che un essere umano non merita, e quindi avendoli sfidati, in qualche modo, sono diventato simbolo e quindi mi è stata data la protezione. Il pericolo non nasce da chi pesca, trova, una nuova notizia, il pericolo nasce da chi la riesce a far passare, da chi rompe la crosta degli addetti ai lavori, da chi riesce a far veicolare dei messaggi, dei racconti'.

6. Italian original: 'la trasformazione di una vicenda essenzialmente mediale in un *morality play*, in cui si scontrano non punti di vista o categorie analitiche, ma allegorie, ovvero simboli personificati: in primo luogo l'Eroe contro il Crimine (con varianti quali il Santo contro il Maligno o il Martire contro i Persecutori).

7. During a TV appearance in the programme *Otto e Mezzo* on channel La7, Saviano clarifies what he means by 'trend' with reference to the struggle against the camorra. The writer explains it is a provocation to invite the readers to be inspired by any kind of curiosity (e.g. about the book, the writer, the TV show) in order to know and understand the mechanisms regulating politics and the criminal economy. Saviano admits this might be risky, as the public attention may be superficial and may not lead to the change of the state of things, and yet, in his view, this has not happened yet, as the young generations have shown the desire of knowing more and more about these complex issues.

8. To say the truth, it is worthy to note that in a long and detailed article titled *L'uomo che sparò all'autore di Gomorra (Smells Like Skunky Spirit)*, published by the blog *Carmilla. Letteratura Immaginario e cultura di opposizione*, the blog editors accuse Dal Lago of 'leaving out' and 'counterfeiting' the sources of his research, and they denounce the 'incredible editorial slovenliness of Dal

Lago's text, as well as the lack of proof-check of his statements. (https://www.carmillaonline.com/2010/06/22/luomo-che-spar-allautore-di-gomorra/, accessed 12 October 2016).

Italian original: 'In un paese in cui la diffusione della conoscenza è largamente appaltata ai media e i conflitti ridotti a stereotipi, che a guidare l'opposizione morale al crimine organizzato sia lo scrittore-eroe appare del tutto coerente. Quando Saviano dice che la sua missione . . . è creare una moda, ammette semplicemente di voler promuovere un egalitarismo unanimista e di maniera: Mondadori ha pubblicato il suo libro, gran parte dei quotidiani lo sponsorizzano e tutti sono contenti. I lettori di destra, centro e sinistra, dopo aver letto *Gomorra*, si convinceranno di aver contribuito alla lotta contro il crimine organizzato, potranno dormire sonni tranquilli e tornare alle loro occupazioni. Ma, come è noto, le mode vanno e vengono'.

9. By text I mean here 'Roberto Saviano' as a public persona, 'a web of textual meanings, a contested site, a sign constructed socially, by himself [*sic*], by the publisher, and his [*sic*] readers' (O'Reilly quoted in Bassi 2015: 3).

10. Quotation taken from Paul Bowman's essay in the original language: 'The Task of the Transgressor', in *Culture Machine*, n.6 (2004). Available at: http://www.culturemachine.net/index.php/cm/article/viewArticle/6.

11. Quotation taken from Paul Bowman's essay in the original language, *For a New Intervention*, unpublished in English.

THREE

Gomorrah: Event, (con)text, reviews

The task of the writer and the magic of words

A DISRUPTIVE EVENT

Roberto Saviano's first meaningful intervention was definitely *Gomorrah*. What happened when this book was published in 2006 was an event and a disruptive intervention in different realms: journalism, literature, media, pop culture and politics, namely the spaces of connection and articulation and the domains of struggle and challenge to the several forms of cultural hegemony and dominant discourses. As it is evident since the first emails written to his editor Edoardo Brugnatelli (2016), while still conceiving of his book, Roberto Saviano declared a strong 'will to connect' (Hall 2001: 263), anxiously trying to make a difference in Italy. He wanted the country to know what was happening in a relatively small area of the nation, Campania, because this was having huge effects on the real lives of all citizens on a global scale:

> the desire to write this book arises from the anger moulded day after day staring at these new and unknown 'Principles of entrepreneurship' and recollecting the people massacred without getting any attention, as their lives were minor lives.[1] (Saviano 29/11/2004 in Brugnatelli 2016, my translation from Italian)

As we are going to see, *Gomorrah* and its author are texts and discourses which have broken the conventions and boundaries of literary genres, thus changing the representation and the resulting people's perception of the issues discussed, operating within mainstream media in the attempt of modifying their agenda as well as, even more importantly, the agenda of politics. This is the reason why Roberto Saviano's work can be considered as a form of alterdisciplinary intervention with a clear ethical-political vocation. Indeed, as defined by Paul Bowman, the aim of alterdisciplinarity is 'to intervene into and to alter *other* disciplinary discourses and their productions (knowledges) not by critiquing them but by intervening into the disciplinary spaces of their production and legitimation – that is: getting inside knowledge, undoing methodologies and arguing in the other's language for other conclusions' (Bowman 2011: 67). This is what, in my view, Roberto Saviano concretely does.

Saviano opens his successful first book with this dedication: 'To S., damn it'. Pronouncing these words repeatedly, with a special stress on 'damn', they sound like a scream that starts reverberating in 2006, the year of the publication of the book and echoes until today. The loud and obsessive sound you can fancy to hear marks two destinies of damnation, inextricably intertwined: first the ruin brought to Naples by intimidation, corruption, drug trafficking, toxic waste and murders, described in the non-fiction novel; and second, Saviano's destiny of damnation, an inexorable journey towards the loss of his physical liberty (October 2006) that he undertook after something unexpected happened: the mechanisms of the modern camorra gained the interest of worldwide audiences.

With more than five million copies of the book sold, in Italy and abroad, translated into several languages, Roberto Saviano's non-fiction novel *Gomorrah* becomes a literary phenomenon of astonishing proportions. Before *Gomorrah,* in Italy many books had dealt with the same issue, mafias, yet so far only Saviano's book has reached such a triumphal success. For the writer Helena Janeczek, formerly a Mondadori editor, the editor of *Gomorrah* itself and a blogger for *Nazione Indiana,*

> *Gomorrah* is no doubt the first book on mafias . . . to have a similar spread in Italy and in the world. *Gomorrah* has changed the way of representing and seeing mafias: no longer a local phenomenon, but a ubiquitous presence intertwined with the globalized

> world; no longer a tangle of criminal and political power, but the supremacy of the economic power to which all the rest is subdued. (Janeczek 2008, my translation from Italian)

Hence, *Gomorrah* has altered the representation of mafias, as it does not deal with the camorra in abstract terms, but it quotes real names and places, and describes vividly the people and their businesses. In this way, the audience realizes the extent of the problem and how it affects the smallest things in their everyday life, for instance, the functioning of the clothing and shoe manufacturing; the illegal commercial network of high-tech products imported from the Chinese market; the distribution of goods, their retail chain and prices and the pollution caused by toxic waste drained into the lands where food products eaten by citizens are grown. Moreover, in *Gomorrah* Saviano manages to deconstruct the mythology of mafia heroes describing and narrating not only powerful epic moments in their life, such as summit meetings, killings, shiny cars or gorgeous women, as shown in classic movies like *The God father*, but above all displaying their miserable daily existence, the smell of their money and their hunted life.

THE LITERARY CONTEXT

Genealogy of an international success

The literary context where *Gomorrah* bursts into is, first and foremost, that of the emergent trend of an online literary realm mostly made up of blogs and webzines. Initially (late 1990s–2005), this was an alternative and 'illegitimate' space where the critique to the official cultural and editorial system was allowed and welcomed, while after the first years of 2000 this online literary realm reached its legitimation, institutionalization and even 'domestication', thus losing its polemical *vis*. As Lombardi outlines (2016), the first and probably most emblematic experience in the Italian literary web is *Nazione Indiana*, a blog founded in 2003 almost as the direct consequence of a conference held in Milan in November 2001, titled *Scrivere sul fronte occidentale* (Writing on the Western Front). The main objective of the conference organizers, Antonio Moresco and Dario Voltolini, was to discuss a widespread sense of awkwardness, as writers, *vis-à-vis* the images of the September 11 attacks to the Twin

Towers in New York, which appeared to decree (also) the collapse of a long-lasting age of fixity and crystallization in the arts, literature and culture. For most of the authors who took part in that conference, the old paradigms of interpretation were no longer fit for the contemporary world:

> We look silently at the repeated images of the first plane going in, then of the second one. They repeatedly go in the towers and make them repeatedly crumble. Together with some friends with whom a relationship of debate and regard has started, I feel the need to confront with all this as a writer too. . . . I need this for a feeling of invasion and communion, because things are entangled; because it seems to me that this dramatic start of the new century and millennium throws away all the little ideologies and conceptual and theoretical obsessions which have kept the arts, knowledge and thinking imprisoned for decades.[2] (Lombardi 2016)

When *Nazione Indiana* was launched, its first contributors – all writers except one literary critic, Carla Benedetti – were determined to continue the controversy with the literary establishment and the traditional literary critique, accused of being asphyctic and asphyxiating, and to revenge the fundamental role of writers as agents of social change. The web then appeared to be the best space, both collective and independent, to dismantle the old fixity of roles and ideas, and to experiment with styles, genres and issues.

Roberto Saviano was one of the contributors to *Nazione Indiana*: he soon proved to be an *engagé* writer, an excellent example of the new cultural and literary vision promoted by the blog founders and, because of this, much appreciated by the readers and blog commentators from the very moment his reportages about the camorra were posted online in June 2003. Saviano managed to catalyse much of the visitors' traffic to the *Nazione Indiana* website and, at the same time, he also managed to get the attention of the offline community. The publication of *Gomorrah,* in 2006, marked the official sanction both of *Nazione Indiana* as a key literary hub and of the wider online literary scene (Lombardi 2016).

Nevertheless, around 2005, some of the founders and main contributors to *Nazione Indiana* decided to stop writing for the blog. Thus, they provoked a rupture in the collective and caused the birth of the second generation of online literary experiences, like 'Il primo amore', 'minima&moralia', 'doppiozero' and 'Le parole e le cose', which were – and still are – perfectly integrated into the official literary realm (Lombardi 2016). The rupture within the community of *Nazione Indiana* mainly followed a highly polemical debate on the true literary value of bestsellers and the new publishing market, which Carla Benedetti defined as 'the industry of the cultural genocide' (Lombardi 2016).

The genre and the body

A similar polemical debate involved the New Italian Epic, a corpus of works also including *Gomorrah*. New Italian Epic (hence NIE) is a label coined by writer Wu Ming 1[3] in a workshop on Italian literature given at the McGill University of Montreal in 2008, later discussed in other North American universities including Boston MIT, and finally formalized into a memorandum.[4] Wu Ming 1 defines the NIE as a corpus, or 'nebula', of recent books ('New'), written in the Second Republic – particularly between 1993 and 2008 – which are very different one from another. They are almost 'unidentified literary objects', yet sharing fundamental elements, such as the merging of creative writing with non-fictional documents such as letters, journalistic reports and judicial transcriptions, combined with an essentially allegorical nature (2008: 3). This is true also for *Gomorrah*, where Roberto Saviano picks up information from *archives* and from the *streets*, two special sources of information from most of NIE authors. Particularly, according to Dimitri Chimenti, in *Gomorrah* there is a 'narrative capitalisation of archives' since the quotations from the texts belonging to an extradiegetic time, such as the aforementioned non-fictional documents useful to retrace events and characters of the recent history, are made understandable thanks to the literary fiction itself (Chimenti 2010).

The reaction of literary critics to the NIE was vibrant and variegated: Alberto Asor Rosa welcomed it as the only recent attempt of giving Italian contemporary literature a theoretical-literary arrangement worthy of the name (Wu Ming 2009: 60), while Pierpaolo Antonello, for instance, defined it simply as a cool rebranding of the postmodern poetics (2012: 31). Nevertheless, the NIE focuses on a subject matter deserving critics' attention, according to Maurizio Vito. In his view, the NIE

> has already made an encouraging impact on some cultural apparatuses of literary Italy. . . . Particularly, it has shaken a distracted audience and revitalized a sluggish and uniform contemporary tradition of critical theorizing, providing readers as well as authors with an opportunity to reinvent their roles and engage in social and political understanding. (Wu Ming 1 2010: 410)

As Wu Ming 1 clarifies, all the NIE works tell about our contemporary age, an age of uncertainties, missed legacies, structural crisis and imminent catastrophes. Hence the poetics underlying the NIE deals with a strong ethical and epic vocation, often facing issues like postcolonialism and subalternity – mostly perceived as marginal in Italy – in the attempt of writing stories both experimental and popular, disrupting the boundaries of literary genres.

Therefore, the word 'epic' in the label NIE not only refers to the great choral narrations, sagas and long-time stories full of characters where the collective destinies of entire nations, classes and ethnic communities are at play, but it also means 'promise', 'pledge', 'prophecy', in its Greek sense. This is the reason why, in their novels, the writers of the NIE show an assumption of responsibility and a vision for the future, especially because the aim of literature today should be the challenge to reality. They show a great trust in 'the maieutic and telepathic power of words' and 'their ability to establish relationships', namely a kind of trust which may engender new practices among 'the multitude' (2010).

And it was a multitude of students who, in November 2010, demonstrated in the streets of Rome against the draft law on University and Education signed by Mariastella Gelmini, a minister of Silvio Berlusconi's government. The students leading the demonstration became known as 'Book Blocks', as they wore coloured plastic shields to defend themselves from the police attacks. On those shields they wrote the names and titles of some classics of literature and philosophy, thus performing a highly symbolic 'tactic'. As it has been observed, the only Italian titles on the shields belonged to the 'nebula' of the NIE, such as *Q* by Luther Blissett, *Noi saremo tutto* by Valerio Evangelisti, *In ogni caso nessun rimorso* by Pino Cacucci, *Asce di Guerra* by Wu Ming and, last but not the least, *Gomorrah*. According to Wu Ming 1, this is a relevant detail if we think in terms of the ability of these works to 'establish relationships' and engender trust in the maieutic potential of writing. It is clear, in fact, that on that occasion the students chose the books that, more than others, were meaningful to them and carried appropriate messages for their struggle. Those books reflected an assumption of responsibility on the part of their authors, striving for the readers so that they could perceive the writers' commitment in changing reality:

> an idea clear enough of the authors' involvement in their work, of the weight of words, of the responsibility towards the people who will read it seeking something 'touching' in it, something relevant, a spark of truth. 'Assumption of responsibility' means working hard, it means putting your heart and soul in your work and doing your best so that the reader can understand that commitment, the effort to gain his/her respect without taking it for granted.[5] (Vito 2011: 8)

The most frequent definition of the literary genre *Gomorrah* belongs to, however, is hybrid or non-fiction novel. As Clotilde Bertoni (2009) points out, this is a difficult narrative category to explain, largely undefinable, although there are two main possible interpretations of it. The former, usually referring back to Truman Capote and his work *In Cold Blood* first printed in 1965 designates a branch which developed together with new journalism in the 1960s and consisted of a narrative elaboration or a free use of authentic materials and sources collected with journalistic methods. The latter, instead, includes all those genres basically founded on reality, such as memoranda, autobiographies, autofictions (namely new autobiographical pacts where the protagonist is not the author but his or her projection): that is to say all those genres combining truth and fiction and sometimes including the slant of essays. As Bertoni puts it commenting on *Gomorrah*, Saviano's work has gained such a huge interest because it has freed the information taken from judicial transcriptions and trials from its aseptic and impersonal tone, using in the narrative the filter of the involved subjectivity of the narrator (75–76), of his carnal knowledge of events and his bodily reaction to the daily cruelty of criminal power. Below we can read an example taken from the chapter 'The Secondigliano War':

> I went home, but I couldn't sit still. I went out again and started to run, faster and faster, my knees gyrating, my heels drumming my buttocks, my arms flailing like a puppet's. My heart was

> pounding, my tongue and teeth were drowning in saliva. I could feel the blood swelling in the veins in my neck, flooding my chest, I was out of breath, inhaling all the air I could and then exhaling hard, like a bull. I started running again, my hands frozen, my face on fire, my eyes closed. I felt I had absorbed all the blood I had seen on the ground, that all the blood that had gushed out, as if from a broken faucet, was now pumping through my body. (Saviano 2008e: 121)

Now, for Bertoni, even if Saviano has stumbled in some flaws, such as patheticism in some cases and the use of ventured metaphors and similes in others, these flaws have not ruined the overall effect of the narration. Hence once more, as we have seen in the previous chapter, the role of the author/narrator's body in *Gomorrah* is clearly crucial. It is so imperfect and partial that it does not guarantee the possibility of a pure knowledge, explains Palumbo Mosca, but at the same time it is a guarantor of the narrator's sincerity on which the reliability of the narration is based. According to Palumbo Mosca, 'The body reacquires veracity and specificity because it is the signifier of the presence in the world of the author-narrator and his engagement in what is recounted. Consequently, the body is not estranged as an object of knowledge, instead it is assumed to be a knowing subject' (2015: 10). Particularly, continues Palumbo Mosca, in *Gomorrah* 'the tendency to represent emotions and, more generally, abstract situations in corporeal terms is linked to the principle that information or interpretation can be inexact or misused, whereas the body does not lie' (10).

The body does not lie and the emotional involvement of the author-narrator in the narrative is a fundamental moment in the new dynamics of engagement and ethical-political intervention (see Palumbo Mosca 2009), as it provokes the awareness of the relevance of the narrated events in the readers and offers them the tools for the social and political change. It is not by chance, then, that Roberto Saviano thinks deeply about how to structure his book giving it a more unitary and uniform structure exactly thanks to a narrative voice in first person 'who does not chart his own diary', but 'a memory of the place', choosing to write neither a merely fictional narration nor a thriller. As Saviano states, 'I'd like to plot this narration in first person, neither searching for the separation from fiction, nor making it usable as a thriller'[6] (Saviano in Brugnatelli 2016, my translation from Italian). Finally, as Wu Ming 1 has suggested

(2006), in *Gomorrah* 'Roberto Saviano' – the first person narrator – is not just the author Roberto Saviano, but a multiple point of view, estranged and, at the same time, firm in the sense of coherence and morally good. The 'I' in *Gomorrah* is a collective voice expressing the words and feelings of a community as a whole, especially of that part of the community which is still brave enough to find an 'unassailable root' to stare the criminal powers in the face: 'Christ, Buddha, civil commitment, ethics, Marxism, pride, anarchy, the fight against crime, cleanliness, persistent and everlasting rage, southerness. Something' (Saviano 2008e: 232). *Gomorrah*, for Wu Ming 1, is a tribute to all those 'something'.

THE GREY ZONE OF ITALIAN JOURNALISM

Without any doubt, *Gomorrah* has attracted the readers' attention for all the reasons I have explained so far. Nevertheless, it is also true that it has filled a sort of empty space in the Italian news system. Despite Italy is penetrated by mafias, a large part of journalism deals with the camorra (and with mafias in general) as criminal organizations;[7] it hardly ever denounces and points out the connections between mafias, politics and businesses. This means that the audience is usually informed about criminal events, above all murders, but it is never guided to understand the power of mafias in depth: their ideology, politics, economy. Let's see why.

First, it is worthy to know that until a few years ago, mafias were supposed to operate only in some southern Italian regions, especially Sicily, Calabria, Campania, Apulia and Basilicata. However, after 15 November 2010 (the date of a speech-tale Roberto Saviano gave on TV during the show *Vieni via con me*), the perception that mafia issues also affect the north of Italy has become evident. That was the day of another great disruptive intervention Saviano carried out in mainstream media, provoking a political and cultural debate in the society. In that show, Saviano denounced the massive presence of criminal affairs in the north of Italy. Particularly, he denounced the presence of 'Ndrangheta in Lombardy arousing harsh polemics with Roberto Maroni, the region governor representative of Lega Nord, a political party accused of supporting criminal organizations, like all other parties when holding the power. As Saviano stated,

> It is in the North that criminal organizations, especially 'ndrangheta, do business. Lombardy is the region with the highest rate of criminal investments in Europe. 'Ndrangheta infiltrates in Lombardia's economy, health system, politics. In this sense, Milan is the capital of criminal affairs. Suffice it to take a city map to highlight all the tenders and works controlled or infiltrated by criminal mobs, in this case 'ndrangheta: Santa Giulia, Milan Navigli Euro, Milan-Bergamo Tav, Milan-Bergamo motorway, Central Station, new courthouse, Portello, City Life, Porta Garibaldi, Milan-Rho Fair, metro line 5, ex Ansaldo area, Atm town police warehouse, Corvetto area, customs agency.[8] (2010b: 67–68)

In 2007, when this awareness had not been achieved yet, the seminars organized by *Libera Informazione* in the southern Italian regions proved that some of the most problematic issues concerning Italian journalism were the financial, industrial and political conflicts of interest at regional and national levels; the pressure on editors; the exploitation of young journalists without a contract or with a temporary one; the intimidating use of civil reparation against journalists, censorships and self-censorships. As Chiara Spagnolo denounced, a journalist then writing for *Quotidiano di Calabria*, 'In Italy politicians love the silence on their businesses and many journalists normally practice it' (Morrione 2008: 50, my translation from Italian). The most appealing news in Italy are those concerning private and horrific crimes, like that of young student Meredith Kercher's murder in Perugia, for instance. Investigative journalism, instead, usually emerges only when criminal organizations reach the climax of their violence, namely when they 'do pieces', when they murder someone, especially well-known people like judges Giovanni Falcone and Paolo Borsellino killed in the 1990s. Few people care that 'the strategy of infiltration of criminal organizations is the more effective the more the Mobs manage to avoid clamorous events', as Roberto Morrione points out (2008: 190).

In his speech at the seminar organized by *Libera Informazione* in Campania, Enzo Palmesano – a freelance journalist collaborating at that time with a local newspaper, and then made redundant in 2015 (see Saviano 2015b) – explained how the camorra can use the power of communication very well, trying to subdue it to its interests. As Palmesano proves, the criminal mobs control two out of three local newspapers of the area around Caserta, influencing their language, contents and messages. As we will see further on in this book, Roberto Saviano has spoken about this manipulation of information on different occasions: during the *Festival della Letteratura* of Mantua in 2008, in the TV programme *Che tempo che fa* in 2009 and then in his book *La parola contro la camorra* in 2010. Focusing on the local newspapers *Il Corriere di Caserta, Cronache di Napoli* and *la Gazzetta di Caserta,* Saviano analyses their titles, language and pictures which seem to anesthetize the readers' conscience and make them accustomed to the 'banality of evil' and to the passive acceptance of the existing state of things (2010b).

As a matter of fact, among the traditional features assigned to people living in a place affected by mafias is their conspiracy of silence, their 'omertà', which is the vehicle for a hopeless and resigned world view. In *Gomorrah* Saviano states that truth is almost never stated in his land, because

> living as if you actually believe truth can exist is incomprehensible. So the people around you feel uncomfortable, undressed by the gaze of one who has renounced the rules of life itself, which they have fully accepted. And accepted without feeling ashamed, because in the end that's how things are and have always been; you can't change it all on your own, and so it's better to save your energy, stay on track, and live the way you're supposed to live. (2008e: 280)

And yet the best results of the struggle against mafias cannot be attributed to the state, which has often impeded these fights, but to a 'composite group of representatives of the public opinion, people working within the institutions and politicians, probably in the minority in the three sectors' (Caselli in Morrione 2008: 11, my translation from Italian). Hence this is the importance of a massive work of 'denuncia', commitment, bravery, resistance, social and political agency, which may prevent resignation, described by Saviano as follows:

> When everything possible has been done, when talent, skill, ability, and commitment are fused in a single act, when all this isn't enough to change anything, then you just want to lie down, stretch out on nothing, in nothing. To vanish slowly, let the minutes wash over you, sink into them as if they were quicksand. To do nothing but breath. (2008e: 35)

READING *GOMORRAH* ABROAD...

In the Oscar Mondadori edition of *Gomorrah* (2010), the publisher decided to include a section titled *Gomorra nel mondo* collecting an anthology of the most meaningful reviews, comments and analysis of the non-fiction novel published abroad between 2007 and 2009. These articles show that foreign newspapers and magazines – American, Swedish, British, German, Greek, Spanish, Croatian, Brasilian, Israeli and Albanian – agree in highlighting the incredible power of denunciation and civil reaction that *Gomorrah* generated. In their opinion, the book radically changed the way of perceiving Italy and the global market. The *New York Times*, for instance, defines Saviano's book as 'part economic analysis, part social history, part *cri de coeur*', a 'crushing testimonial' and 'the most important book to come out of Italy in years' (Saviano 2010a: 360–365). For the *Stockholms Fria*, instead, *Gomorrah* is a book 'you can't stop thinking at' (369), while for *El País* it is 'an extraordinary reportage on mafias . . . which leaves you as fascinated as incredulous' (378). Moreover, for *Shkirimi Shqup*, an Albanian newspaper, '*Gomorrah* is a manual of bravery', and Saviano is a writer who has broken the silence with his words'. As the journalist writes, Roberto Saviano, defined by Umberto Eco as 'the national conscience of Italy', is also 'the national conscience of Albania',

> not only because he speaks about criminal organizations, but above all because he speaks about freedom. Few people dare to do this in my land. Saviano, instead, has spoken to Albanian people about courage, revolt, anger and indignation. He has spoken about possibilities and hope. . . . In a country that will be destroyed by silence and buried by indifference, in a country where words are losing their power and meaning, Saviano has spoken and has urged to speak. (392; my translation from Italian)

The comparative reflection between the reality portrayed by *Gomorrah* and that of one's own country is one of the key elements also in the *Globes* review, an Israeli newspaper, while the German *Frei Presse* hints at the 'glimmer of hope' in the 'apocalyptic scenario' narrated by Saviano traceable in the brave witnesses of the people who denounce the criminal mobs.

Vis à vis the unanimity in the global reception of *Gomorrah,* it is good to ask what is, for the readers, the shattering strength of this book, which many have considered as a watershed in Italian and world literature. To do this, I have analysed the readers' reviews of *Gomorrah* collected on Amazon.com, one of the best-known multinational e-commerce and bookstore companies. Particularly, my enquiry focuses on the textual analysis of the reviews of *Gomorrah*'s English translation for the American market by Virginia Jewiss (*Gomorrah: A Personal Journey into the Violent International Empire of Naples' Organized Crime System*, 2008e), including a reader sample from different countries: Greece, Austria, Malta, but especially the USA. At present, the Amazon average customer assigns four appreciation stars out of five to the translation of *Gomorrah*.[9] More precisely, the web page displays 181 comments: the 73 per cent of them express top positive opinions (four or five stars), while only the 17 per cent express critical opinions (one or two stars). The readers' debate on Amazon is very lively and mainly focuses on the author's approach to the subject matter, the language, the narrative thread, the characters' insight and the quality of the translation of *Gomorrah*.

Far from being a work of objective and analytic journalism, *Gomorrah* is considered by many reviewers as an 'act of bravery' and as a 'compelling, excellent, fabulous and magnificent book', conveying 'a fascinating and unique perspective on the world today'. For a large part of the audience, *Gomorrah* is a book written with passion in a punchy writing style, so one must get used to the style to breathe the breathlessness Roberto Saviano tries to convey. Furthermore, the readers think that 'the feeling of sick indignation is palpable in each sentence', and according to them, using intelligence and heart, Roberto Saviano has a way with words that at times sounds like poetry. Talented as a writer, curious as a journalist and with an intense love for his hometown, for many reviewers the author simply tries to understand what is happening around him and to explain why things are the way they are.

Of course, the readers' negative reviews in some cases clearly contradict the opinions listed earlier; therefore the main critiques to Saviano's narration mainly concern the translation and the narrative thread. Apart from a few contrasting opinions, according to which both the author and the translator deserve credit since the high level of prose is elegantly maintained throughout the book, many readers declare they found themselves 'lost in translation'. They maintain the English translation does not come through clearly, being 'stark and breathless' with a 'spare and unadorned' writing. Besides, the readers state that the translation lacks some critical elements that would help to make the story more than a timeline of crime.[10] Particularly, according to some readers, the narration lacks a clear timeline and fluency, as well as a deep insight into the characters' minds, so that the readers carry out a 'boring' and 'heartless' reading. For instance, a reader from the USA states, 'There is no narrative thread. There are no characters you can organize your emotions around, so the whole thing is ultimately heartless', while a reader from the UK points out that the narration is not credible, and the author lacks authority and expertise into mafias:

> *P. (UK)*: Roberto Saviano has absolutely no insight into the Mafia. This is certainly not an authoritative account of the Mafia, nor is it a good read, indeed 'extremely tedious' is the best way to describe this book. The information is barely credible, the claims of prosecutors who knew very little, interviews with police, probably all collected second hand from newspapers and TV News. I am not an expert on the Mafia or literature on the Mafia, but there must be many books that offer real insight. This is not one of them.

In addition, according to a part of the readers, the 'dizzying array of names', 'the tedious overuse of allegory and metaphor', as well as the mention of 'too many details, although quite revealing', cause 'problems of readability': they define *Gomorrah* as a 'good story, poorly told', and as a 'wasted opportunity'. Nevertheless, some of these much disapproved stylistic choices – for instance, the dizzying array of names – have been functional to Saviano's act of 'denuncia', the essential aim of his narration. On the contrary, the positive reactions highlight the beginning of a fundamental cultural process involving the readers' transformation, the awareness that our world view cannot stay the same after reading *Gomorrah*, and, as a consequence, the importance of taking side.

. . . AND IN ITALY

The Gomorrah/*Saviano hype*

Recent research conducted by Edoardo Brugnatelli and Chiara Faggiolani (2016) on the digital traces *Gomorrah*'s readers have left on the Italian community of the social reading platform aNobii from 2007 to 2016 shows that this feeling of transformation is much more evident in the Italian reception of the book, probably influenced by the higher popularity of the writer in Italy.

Their study object is the corpus of *Gomorrah*'s reviews – made up of 1.395 comments – examined by means of an objective analysis carried out using statistical techniques, information retrieval and computational linguistics. The research also includes references to some meta-information, such as the gender of the readers/reviewers; their age; their geographical area of origin; the number of reviews written on aNobii and finally their popularity, in terms of number of followers, on the same platform.

As Faggiolani points out, one of the most frequent words, or 'types', in the reviews is the verb *dovere* (must/have to) with all its inflections, followed by others like *raccontare* (tell), *capire* (understand), *parlare* (speak), *riuscire* (manage), *pensare* (think), *vedere* (see), *sentire* (feel), *conoscere* (know), *credere* (believe), *trovare* (find), *mettere* (put). Moreover, a sub-corpus analysis of the word cloud around *dovere* (must/have to) reveals that the readers use this verb in many ways. For instance, they refer to the urgence of telling what the camorra and its implications are, the necessity or duty to continue this *denuncia* thanks to Saviano's book, literature and journalism and finally the necessity to make *Gomorrah* a mandatory reading in schools, so that things could finally change in the country. In this sense, as Faggiolani writes, *Gomorrah* 'is perceived as a book that must be read and that had to be written and defended' (2016). It may be interesting to observe that the focus on this sense of duty, the urgence of 'denuncia', the truth revealed by the book, as well as the bravery of the writer is more emphasized by female and young readers (15–24 years old), while male readers prefer to highlight the features related to the book characters, setting and themes. Furthermore, while there are no meaningful differences in the book reviews written by very active and popular readers/reviewers on aNobii and readers coming from different geographical areas within Italy, it is interesting to notice that people leaving abroad, although writing in Italian, use words like *rabbia* (anger), *doloroso* (painful) and *tristezza* (sadness) with much more specificity.

This research by Brugnatelli and Faggiolani is really engaging as it concretely shows the animated relationship between *Gomorrah* and its readers since its publication, but also because it witnesses the readers' changing perceptions towards Roberto Saviano as a writer first, and as a symbol later. Particularly, Edoardo Brugnatelli refers how, despite the approval of the book has remained unvaried, the contents of the reviews change progressively throughout the years. Brugnatelli analyses these changes adapting the principles of the so-called Hype cycle[11] to the *Gomorrah*/Roberto Saviano cultural mass phenomenon in order to measure their popularity and coolness over time. What Brugnatelli finds out is that the focus and tone of the reviews shift from the book *Gomorrah* to the author/symbol Roberto Saviano over time; but also, more importantly, he proves how the general perception of a book as a mass and marketing phenomenon can have a strong influence on the readers' reception, sometimes inhibiting its fruition. As Brugnatelli shows, after the climax of the *Gomorrah*/Saviano hype or enthusiasm (years 2008/2009), a period of backlash followed (years 2011–2013), totally changing the perception of the book/author from their highest value, coolness and popularity to negative reception and even a sense of banality and vacuity associated to the cultural products in question. However, even after winning the resistance against the overexposure and supposed marketing plot involving *Gomorrah*/Roberto Saviano, their audience still finds the reading necessary and mandatory for everyone in Italy, as the following review reported by Brugnatelli demonstrates:

> When the book came out, I didn't want to hear a thing about it. I hate those books arousing too much noise, trends and marketing around them. I have decided to read it only recently, after following the writer's various statements and vicissitudes for years. Although I don't like trendy books, I'm left with curiosity to satisfy anyway. Therefore, last summer I made up my mind and bought it. It is a necessary-reading, a reading everyone in Italy should face.[12] (8 October 2015)

After the release of *Gomorra. La Serie* in 2014, now at its third season, the *Gomorrah*/Saviano hype is experiencing a new coolness, although weaker than at the time of its climax. Nobody knows what will happen to this hype in the future, but for the moment suffice it to say that the aNobii Italian community has decreed *Gomorrah* as the second most-voted book after *Siddartha* by Herman Hesse and before many other classics and bestsellers, such as *The Catcher in the Rye* by Salinger and *The Kite Runner* by Hosseini. This is definitely one of the possible demonstrations of its relevance, influence and transformative nature for the readers' identity.

THE TASK OF THE WRITER

Previously in this chapter, I have highlighted the importance of the emotional and bodily involvement of Roberto Saviano in his narration, which is, at the same time, both the guarantee of the sincerity of the author-narrator and of the credibility of the narration itself. As also shown by the readers' reviews to *Gomorrah*, the writer's deep emotional investment in the subject matter is not a limit of Saviano's writing. It represents, instead, his core idea of literature and of the writer's task, which can be plainly read in many texts presenting Saviano's contributions, such as William Grimes's article for The *New York Times* (2007), or in different fragments of articles published in *La Bellezza e l'Inferno* (2009c).[13]

For instance, Saviano declares to Grimes that he believes that 'the way to truly understand, to get to the bottom of things, is to smell the hot breath of reality, to touch the nitty-gritty'. As he states, when you write, you have to 'look simultaneously at the hell of humankind and at the wonders that flow out from its pulsating life' (Saviano 2009c; English trans: 51); 'you need to be able to distance yourself, to take leaps, to stop, and most of all to do battle, to fight without having to beat anyone, to trigger new movements, to make energy jump off the page, not shut itself in' (52).

Saviano's aim is not just that of writing a good book, construct a story and polish words until an elegant and recognizable style is achieved (9); he declares to be not interested in 'literature as a vice', nor in 'literature as a lesser philosophy'. He does not care 'about beautiful stories that cannot be bothered to deal with the blood of our time'; rather, he wants to 'smell the rot of politics and the stench of business' (266). Making reference to Hemingway, Saviano maintains that style is fundamental but 'the writer's grace, sense of time and profundity all need to be held hostage by the pressure of the situation, by the need to be spoken, to be revealed' (266). Hence for Saviano, the act of writing

> is a way of inscribing [his] words on the world, of passing them on like a clandestine message; one of those notes you have to

> read, memorize and destroy: chew it up, let your saliva break it down, so the message is properly digested. Writing is a form of resistance; writing *is* resisting (9).

The task of the writer is to abuse every tool available to him (267), and to believe that words, spoken publicly and clearly, have not exhausted their resources and power, the power of intervening in the mechanisms of things. For example, this is what Saviano most appreciated of Don Peppino Diana, whose story he narrates in *Gomorrah* (2008e: 223). Saviano believes that the pretension to change things is not an ingenuity, and the kind of writing addressed to a very wide audience 'is not a form of posturing fit only for a talking dead' (Saviano 2009c, English translation: 6). For him, only 'cynics see everything in terms of sly manipulation leading to self-improvement' (6), while it is true that his words, in the hands of so many readers, have turned into instruments of change. 'They became *everyone's stories*' (8). Still on his relationship with 'professional writers' marked by cynicism, he states:

> Over time I have come to appreciate just how much I upset those people. They detest my way of writing, being and appearing. They would like me to disappear. They want me to be more discreet. They would much rather I did not lecture at universities or appear on prime-time television. They would much rather that there were only escapism and entertainment on their screens, so they could have the monopoly on seriousness. Over time, I have learned to measure the value of my words by the enemies they make me. When someone tells me that I have been attacked in certain newspapers, by such and such person, or on a particular television show, I know that I have done well. I know that the more people try to shut me up, the more fear my words inspire. . . . All of this really does make me appreciate those who read me without resorting to insult and slander, fabrications and lies. Only a loyal critic can help me grow and improve. The totalitarian mindset that lies behind the cynicism of certain media channels is my worst enemy. (8–9)

'THE MAGIC OF WORDS': READERS' EMPOWERMENT

On many different occasions Roberto Saviano has repeated like a mantra that the riskiness of his words has not derived from what he wrote, but from the people who have read his work. According to Saviano, in fact, the criminal mobs are never afraid of words *in sé*, but they are scared of their diffusion around the world; they fear publicity more than they fear a trial. The criminal mobs do not deny the right of writing and/or speaking, if it is limited to a restricted audience: what must never happen is that audiences become informed, that talk shows reveal the names of their companies. Saviano's case, in a sense, has brought to the renaissance of empathy, the capacity to understand or feel how another person feels or what he or she is experiencing. In this way, the writer's feelings, his anger and indignation, have become the audience's same feelings. It may not be easy to establish if empathy has been the result of a 'personal relationship' between Roberto Saviano, a 'pop idol' like many others, and a passive audience accustomed to the consumption of the cultural industry products. Or, rather, if it has been the effect of the reawakening of one of 'the most marvellous and most often ignored principles of democracy' (Saviano 2009c; English translation: 135), which might also turn into an instrument for the readers' empowerment. The choice may be subject to undecidability, as it depends on the approach one privileges towards the study of Roberto Saviano, both as an author and as a public persona. What is sure, however, is that the role of the audience has been so crucial for Roberto Saviano that he dedicated his second book to his readers. In the opening pages of *La bellezza e l'inferno*, a collection of articles written from 2004 to 2009, he writes:

> This book is dedicated to my readers. It goes out to those who absorbed my words, who passed them on to friends and family, who used my book in schools. To those who gathered in piazzas across Italy to read aloud from it, proving that my story had become everyone's story, because my words had made it so. This collection goes out to all these people, without whom I am not sure I would have been able to carry on, to write and therefore to resist, to exist, to think about the future. My readers reminded me that my life in a bulletproof bubble is, after all, still a life. Without them I would have never received so much attention. I would have never made it on to the front pages or on to prime-time television. If I had not had so many readers who did something to my book – making more than an object to put back on the shelf after reading – none of this would have been granted to me. And if I became a media sensation, it is thanks to my readers. (Saviano 2009c; English translation: 12–13)

On the basis of the features of his intellectual production discussed so far, Roberto Saviano can arguably be considered as an author on the border between journalism and literature. In an interview to Antonio D'Orrico, Saviano states that in his works, from a technical point of view, he tries to convey the ability to sum information up, without renouncing the abundance of adjectives and the typical aspects of Naples's language variety, particularly idioms and lexical choices. Moreover, Saviano declares to use special purpose language, for example, the vocabulary of necropsy reports dominating the tales of what happens after murders, and to include several details which are often useless for journalists because they distract from the news, but fundamental for narrators as they help connoting the news. Above all, however, in the majority of his texts, Saviano's writing is 'transitive' – in Roland Barthes's terms – hence it is productive and functional to knowledge, being focused on reality, as it should always happen in journalism. Nevertheless in *Gomorrah,* which is also a literary book, Roberto Saviano encourages his audience to reflect on issues exceeding the limits of the contemporary world, the *hic et nunc,* such as the meaning and value of moral and civil engagement, as well as the power and agency of literature. Saviano's writing has questioned the foundation of the 'linguistics of silence' (Ponzio 1993), inviting his readers to assume a listening attitude, no longer that of quiet resignation to the common state of things. Saviano encourages his readers to assume an 'active responsive attitude', to use Backtin words, which can transform their understanding of events in ethical and political action, delay it or keep it quiet. This quotation from Backtin will surely clarify this concept:

> When the listener receives and understand the meaning (the language meaning) of speech, he simultaneously takes an active responsive attitude towards it. He either agrees or disagrees with it (completely or partially), augments it, applies it, prepares for its execution, and so on. And the listener adopts this responsive attitude for the entire duration of the process of listening and understanding, from the very beginning. . . . Any understanding of live speech, a live utterance is inherently responsive, although the degree of this activity varies extremely. Any understanding is imbued with response and necessarily elicits it in one form or another: the listener becomes the speaker. . . . Of course an utterance is not always followed by an articulated response. An

> actively responsive understanding of what is read . . . can be directly realized in action . . ., or it can remain, for the time being, a silent, responsive understanding . . . with a delayed reaction. Sooner or later what is heard and actively understood will find its response in the subsequent speech or behavior of the listener. (Ponzio 1993: 144–145)

Therefore, the crucial role of *Gomorrah*'s audience starts from these assumptions, particularly the one that 'sooner or later what is read and actively understood will find its response in the subsequent speech or behavior of the listener'.

But what is there behind this call to action? In other words, what is the *appeal* of Roberto Saviano's speeches and tales based on? As Paul Bowman reminds us, the meaning of the word 'appeal' not only refers to attraction but also denotes the sense of call, hail and interpellation (Bowman 2010: 170). Thus the question is: are we dealing with Althusser's paradigm of interpellation, which is 'a theory about the mechanism of how we become (again and again) certain sorts of subjects'? (Bowman 2011: 117) Or are we dealing with Jacques Ranciere's paradigm, who interprets identification as 'disidentification that displaces us into a political "place" '? Rancière defines this space as 'the aesthetic dimension of the reconfiguration of the relationships between doing, seeing and saying that circumscribe the being-in-common'. As Rancière puts it, this aesthetic dimension is 'inherent to every political or social movement' (Rancière quoted in Bowman 2011: 117; original essay: 23). In this sense, the entrance on the Italian scene of Roberto Saviano can be defined as part of a cultural and political movement we will discuss further on in the book (chapter 5). Thanks to the readers' positioning in a listening attitude, their emotional participation, as well as the identification they are involved in, 'the moral question is not limited to the level of cognition, but it becomes part of the readers' personality' (Yehoshua quoted in Palumbo Mosca 2009: 319; my translation from Italian). As Palumbo Mosca points out, the new relationship between ethics and literature needs to be found within a process in which the text no longer indicates a truth to be accepted, but the readers' *walk* towards the acquisition of a possible truth (320). Writing is hoping, maintains Saviano, 'when you know, you can hope. . . . Every reader is a hope' (Saviano 2009d).

THE AGENCY OF LITERATURE, OR THE CHANGE 'TO COME'

The term 'agency' designates a key notion in cultural studies and involves both the idea of action and that of strength. In its Italian translation, as Patrizia Calefato observes, it cannot leave the Gramscian concept of 'hegemony' out of consideration. Hegemony, in fact, refers to the intellectual and moral direction within a community, a social group or movement, given by cultural and political élites (Calefato in Chow 2004: 11). Hence if we apply the term to the literary realm, and particularly to *Gomorrah,* it may be worthwhile to wonder if Saviano's literary words – in *Gomorrah* and after *Gomorrah* – have built or may build an intellectual and moral direction within the community of his readers and audience, overcoming the rhetoric of the intellectual-hero to whom any responsibility can be delegated. Indeed, the community of his readers and audience should be able to struggle against the power even in the author's *absence*. As an author, Saviano is the subject of his enunciation, whose aim is to be performative, namely to be able to produce or transform a situation. However, to use Derrida's terms, Saviano's 'signature' will work – hence it will be 'readable' and performative – as long as it remains 'repeatable', 'iterable', detached from its actual and present intention of production. As Derrida declares:

> For a writing to be a writing it must continue to 'act' and to be readable even when what is called the author of the writing no longer answers for what he has written, for what he seems to have signed, be it because of temporary absence, because he is dead or, more generally, because he has not employed his absolutely actual and present intention or attention, the plenitude of his desire to say what he means, in order to sustain what seems to be written 'in his name'. (Derrida in Royle 2003)

In this context I would like to interpret Roberto Saviano's *absence* also as the *death of the author,* in Roland Barthes's terms: the author disappears, steps aside, 'dies' and leaves the task to interpret the 'text' he has created to his readers, whom are invited to cross its multiple meanings and possible senses. As for the change of direction and transformation Saviano has observed in Italian society starting from his experience, he writes:

> nobody can say how much a book can change people all the way, or how much a book has really changed the world. There are no proofs. . . . However, what elements can help us to understand that something is changing? Just observing ourselves. Observing how much a book has changed us. . . . For instance, there is a change when you start doing something you didn't use to do before or, conversely, when you stop doing something. . . . You begin looking at the world with different eyes, you look at things more in depth, you analyze the puzzle of life more carefully. Once again, I want to be cautious on this, I don't want to talk about the rhetoric of change which has happened thanks to my pages. I don't know what can really happen. What I know is that when many people have read my books, I have seen something changing. I have seen the media changing, the judiciary system changing, I have seen trials interrupted for ages starting again. This is not my merit, but my readers' merit. This has happened thanks to suggestions and the word of mouth. In this sense, I strongly believe that literature, so odd as the one I write, can really change things in the everyday.[14] (Saviano 2010d, my translation from Italian)

This is what the political nature of literature consists of: the ability to articulate and provide the tools for a change 'to come', to say it in Derrida's terms; a change which can be immediate or 'open' and 'still to be thought', as Derrida once put it. In this sense, intellectuals continue having a crucial task.

NOTES

1. Italian original: 'il desiderio di questo libro nasce dalla rabbia foggiata nel tempo quotidiano fissando in volto questi nuovi e sconosciuti 'Principi dell'imprenditoria' e ricordando chi è stato massacrato in modo spietato senza ricevere nessuna attenzione, come fossero vite minori'.
2. Italian original: 'Guardiamo in silenzio le immagini ripetute del primo aereo che entra, poi del secondo. Entrano ripetutamente dentro le torri e le fanno ripetutamente crollare. Sento la necessità, assieme ad alcuni amici coi quali è iniziato un rapporto di confronto e di stima, di pormi integralmente di fronte a tutto questo anche come scrittore. . . . Per un bisogno di invasione e di comunione, perché le cose sono intrecciate, perché mi sembra che questo drammatico inizio di secolo e di millennio faccia piazza pulita di tutte le piccole ideologie e fissazioni teoriche e concettuali che tengono imprigionata da decenni l'attività artistica, di pensiero e di conoscenza'
3. The real name of Wu Ming 1 is Roberto Bui, a member of the collective of writers (Wu Ming Foundation, formerly Luther Blissett) who became known after the publication of the novel *Q* in 1999.

4. This memorandum has now three published versions: the first appeared online in April 2008, followed by an update in September of the same year (still available at www.carmillaonline.com), while the third version appeared in a collected volume of works entitled *New Italian Epic. Narrativa, sguardo obliquo, ritorno al futuro*, published in 2009 by Einaudi.

5. Italian original: 'un'idea sufficientemente chiara dell'investimento nell'opera, del peso che hanno le parole, della responsabilità nei confronti di chi la leggerà, cercandovi dentro qualcosa che 'tocchi', qualcosa di rilevante, una scintilla di verità. 'Assunzione di responsabilità' significa lavorare sodo, significa metterci l'anima, e significa adoperarsi perché il lettore colga quell'impegno, quel lavoro per guadagnarsi il suo rispetto senza darlo per scontato'.

6. Italian original: 'vorrei tracciare in prima persona questo racconto non cercando la separazione della fiction né di rendere fruibile il tutto con il calco del thriller'.

7. Before moving further on, it may be of some use to clarify the meaning of the terms 'mafia' and 'camorra', which I have been using so far. Both mafia and camorra are secret criminal societies whose main aim is getting favours or money in an illegal way, especially by practicing intimidations, usury and extortions to little and big companies and enterprises. The criminal nature of mafia and camorra is quite similar to other Italian criminal organizations too, such as 'Ndrangheta in Calabria and Sacra Corona Unita in Puglia. What is different is their place of origin and, above all, their size and structure. Mafia arose in nineteenth century in Sicily (South Italy) and developed later on at a national and international level, while the camorra arose in Naples in the same years. As Saviano maintains, for a long time the camorra has remained almost unknown because of the media distraction on Sicilian mafia bombs, which killed – among other people – two great anti-mafia magistrates in 1992, Giovanni Falcone and Paolo Borsellino. However, the camorra is the most solid criminal organization in Europe in terms of memberships. It arose in the South of Italy, but its production and commercial chains are everywhere in the world. The camorra structure is 'horizontal' and 'flexible', pursuing a purely economic role. For this reason, the camorra is more permeable to new alliances with new clans than the Sicilian mafia and the Calabrian 'Ndrangheta. Clans operate as business committees 'to move capital, set up and liquidate companies, circulate money and invest quickly in real estate without geographical restrictions or heavy dependence on political mediation' (Saviano 2008e: 45). However, as Saviano writes, '*camorra* is a non existent word, a term of contempt used by narcs and judges, journalists and scriptwriters; it's a generic indication, a scholarly term, relegated to history. . . . The word clan members use is *System* . . . an eloquent term, a mechanism rather than a structure. The criminal organization coincides directly with the economy, and the dialectic of commerce is the framework of the clans' (38).

8. Italian original: 'È nel Nord che le organizzazioni criminali, soprattutto la 'ndrangheta, fanno i loro affari. La Lombardia è la regione con il più alto tasso di investimenti criminali d'Europa. Lombarda è l'economia in cui si infiltrano, lombarda la sanità, lombarda la politica. Milano, in questo senso, è la capitale degli affari criminali italiani. Basta prendere una cartina della città e mettere in evidenza tutti gli appalti e i lavori "attenzionati" o infiltrati dalle organizzazioni criminali, in questo caso dalla 'ndrangheta: Santa Giulia, Navigli Euro Milano, Tav Milano-Bergamo, autostrada Milano-Bergamo, Stazione centrale, nuovo tribunale, Portello, City Life, Porta Garibaldi, Fiera Milano-Rho, metro linea 5, area ex Ansaldo, deposito vigili Atm, zona Corvetto, agenzia dogane".

9. Reviews available at: https://www.amazon.com/Gomorrah-Personal-Journey-International-Organized/dp/0312427794/ref=sr_1_1?ie=UTF8&qid=1476259781&sr=8-1&keywords=gomorra. Accessed on 4 October 2016.

10. For an accurate cross-cultural analysis of *Gomorra* translation from Italian into English, see Flavia Cavaliere, 'Tra-durre Gomorra lontano dal suo humus originario' (http://www.bibliocamorra.altervista.org/pdf/TRA-DURRE_GOMORRA.pdf).

11. The *Hype cycle*, which is a research methodology elaborated by the Gartner Inc. company showing the effects of a new technology or application in a social system over time, assumes that a *hype* is 'the enthusiastic and strong feeling around new forms of media and technology'. It consists of five phases: (1) Innovation Trigger; (2) Peak of Inflated Expectation; (3) Through of Disillusionment; (4) Slope of Enlightenment; (5) Plateau of Productivity.

12. Italian original: 'Appena uscì non volli neanche saperne del libro. Detesto quei libri che destano troppo rumore, moda e marketing intorno a sé. Mi sono decisa soltanto di recente, dopo aver seguito per anni svariate dichiarazioni e vicissitudini dello scrittore. Sebbene non mi piacciano i libri che fanno tendenza, mi rimane comunque la curiosità da appagare. Così quest'estate mi sono decisa e l'ho acquistato. Si tratta di una lettura necessaria, una lettura che chiunque in Italia dovrebbe affrontare'.

13. English Translation: *Beauty and the Inferno*, first published in the UK in 2011 and in the USA by Verso in 2012.

14. Italian original: 'nessuno può dire quanto un libro possa fino in fondo cambiare le persone o quanto un libro abbia realmente cambiato il mondo. Non c'è una prova. . . . Però attraverso quali elementi in realtà si può arrivare a capire che qualcosa si sta muovendo? Semplicemente attraverso se stessi. Da quanto un libro ci muta. . . . Per esempio, è cambiamento quando si inizia a fare un gesto che prima non facevi, o, viceversa, un gesto che smetti di fare. Un pensiero che ti si ferma perché lo consideri idiota, per esempio dopo aver letto quel tal libro. Inizi a guardare diversamente il mondo, guardi le cose con più profondità, analizzi con più cura gli intarsi della vita. Su questo voglio essere ancora una volta prudente, cioè non voglio parlare della retorica del cambiamento attraverso la mia pagina. Io non so cosa possa realmente succedere. Quello che so attraverso la mia esperienza è che quando i miei libri sono finiti in mano a molte persone ho visto realmente cambiare qualcosa, ho visto cambiare la macchina mediatica, la macchina giudiziaria, ho visto ripartire percorsi fermi da decenni. Questo non l'ho fatto io ma lo hanno fatto le persone che mi hanno letto. Lo hanno fatto le suggestioni, il passaparola e in questo senso sono convinto che la letteratura, così stramba come quella che faccio io, possa davvero nel quotidiano cambiare le cose'.

FOUR

Disseminations

The end justifies the media

DISSEMINATIONS AND WRITINGS

In his tireless attempts to spread and disseminate his ideas and language – meant here as the ability to imagine new possibilities of being-in-the-world – Roberto Saviano has used several forms of *writing*, such as journalism, literature, radio, cinema, theatre, television, TV series and social networks,[1] 'to institute his sign lastingly', as Derrida said (1989: 21). By means of the contamination of the seeds, words and signs that Saviano has been disseminating using all these different forms and writing practices, many messages have been articulated and scattered in multiple directions, assuring the possibility that something could 'happen, develop, communicate, bear fruits' (36; my translation from Italian). As Silvano Petrosino points out in his editorial introduction to the Italian translation of Derrida's *Dissemination*, not only does writing mean to disseminate but also 'to address'. Indeed, if there is writing, there is a practice of addressing: if experiencing the language is writing, then writing is addressing. Hence, Petrosino comments on the *epistolary nature* of every sign in this way:

> Writing, as an experience of language as language, reveals itself as the act of continuously and assiduously corresponding, without any warranty to get to destination, without any assured path

> or name, but not for this without tension, obstinacy, always circulating, being continuously re-launched. (39–40, my translation from Italian)[2]

Now, as we have seen, the question of the 'addressee', 'recipient', 'reader' and, more generally speaking, of the 'audience' is crucial in the deconstruction of the 'media phenomenon Saviano', and in the following paragraphs I am going to discuss it more thoroughly. What is indisputable, however, is Saviano's obstinacy in disseminating his words, despite running the risk connected to this practice of 'seed (sign, word) dispersal' (38), particularly that of media overexposure and consequent possible loss of originality, credibility and hence reliability for the writer.

THE SOUTHERN FRONT: PASSIONS, REPRESENTATIONS AND RESISTANCE

After the publication of *Gomorrah*, Roberto Saviano started his collaboration with some of the most important international newspapers and magazines (*El País*, the *Times*, the *Washington Post*, the *New York Times* and *Time*) and has become one of the most relevant enunciators of Italian *La Repubblica* and *L'Espresso*,[3] where he signs the majority of his articles, gaining more and more visibility before his audience. In semiotic terms, Roberto Saviano's role in the aforementioned newspapers can be variously defined. Particularly, he can be defined as an *enunciator-expert* or *enunciator-commentator*, both for his well-acknowledged authority as an expert in mafia issues and as a public intellectual. However, what is more relevant is his rhetorical ability to orientate the newspapers' assiological framework and, above all, his readers' passional orientation, thus creating a strong relationship with the audience who eagerly follow him with good or bad comments on the newspapers' websites and Facebook pages, and on his personal page on Facebook.

As semiologists Lorusso and Violi state, a journalistic text is the result of five dimensions – expressive, enunciative, narrative, cognitive and passional – producing specific sense effects thanks to their mutual relationships. Particularly, as for the passional dimension, the two scholars maintain that

> passion . . . cannot be reduced only to the superficial linguistic manifestation or to the lexical usages. Certainly, the presence of passional lexemes directly referring to a certain emotion, as well as a high redundancy of adjectives and adverbs – the lexical categories that more markedly convey emotive qualifications –, are the indicators of a passionate speech, but the levels which may contribute to create a pathemic effect are many others, such as the rhythm of narration or the description of a face, an expression, and a behavior. (Lorusso and Violi 2009: 122–123, my translation from Italian)[4]

As it is known, the semiotics of passions – the study field within the semiotic theory of discourse whose major contributors are Herman Parret, Algirdas J. Greimas and Jacques Fontanille – deals with the problem of meaning. Particularly, it deals with how the meaning is articulated in the text and conveyed to the readers thanks to a specific passionate or *pathemic* orientation of the writing subject or the represented subject. According to the theorists of the semiotics of passions, not only is the uttering subject analysed as a narrative or narrating element, but also as a sensitive or sensual subject able to feel *euphoric* (or enthusiastic) feelings or *dysphoric* (or negative) ones.

Reading Saviano's work from the perspective of the semiotics of passions is interesting given the countless examples of passional lexemes referred to emotions, the redundancy of adjectives and adverbs, the punchy rhythm of the narration and the description of faces, facial expressions and behaviours which are dominant in his writing. The following excerpt is just one of the several examples one may make, and, for this reason, it deserves to be quoted at length:

> What generates a scandal is that a writer, the job considered as the most harmless and useless, can suddenly become responsible for a faded and lopsided light, for an infamous gaze blurting what one wants to be concealed, crying what is whispered, translating into syntax and blowing life towards what was dispersed in fragmentary column sentences and judicial sentences. For a writer, the way of engrafting into the real world is telling about it. It is the writer who can guess and imagine what he cannot see. His imagination and guessing, however, do not follow the will of poetic licence, but they're necessary means to approach the truth lying in what he observes: beyond names, documents, sentences, wiretappings. . . . When you tell the readers about a trial,

when you collect crime news, when you listen to wiretappings, you realize that the only way to understand is telling about all this as a part of a body hiding its organs. And suddenly, what everybody knew within the boundaries of certain areas, passing stories mouth to mouth, kneading them with personal details and legends, what ended in news columns, what seemed to be a territory for insiders, the invisible social operators and anti-mafia expert sociologists, becomes the tale of a whole country, the fascinating and dreadful epic of a winning capitalism that has in cement, transports, textile sector, subcontracts, waste, retailing and whatever can generate profit, its own endless territory of conquest. (Saviano 2006a; my translation from Italian)[5]

The idea of resistance structuring and articulating Saviano's view of writing is highly evocative of the performance of a euphoric attitude towards reality, based on the empathy between the reporter and his audience, and characterized by the hope for the change of the current state of affairs. With the deeply interlocutory tone of many of his articles – which often have the narrative structure of letters – rich in driving provocative questions on reality, everyday life, passivity and resignation, Saviano tries to shake emotionally every recipient of his writings, asking explicitly for clear answers.

Here we can read two excerpts from his 'letters'. The first, titled 'Scrivere sul fronte meridionale'/ 'Writing on the southern front', was published on the literary blog *Nazione Indiana* on 17 April 2005, when he was summoned by his town local police for an interview about all he had written on the blog until then. Saviano was then asked to stop writing on what he knew about the camorra, and to start taking part into trials as a witness:

They say if I have to denounce, I will have to do it formally. . . . In other words, I have to risk, stop writing, become part of the trial, no longer an observer. Shortly, they ask me to become part of a question, whereas by means of writing I insist on keeping different positions, describing the whole process, not the single issue. With writing I insist on facing not the power dynamics of single crimes often I don't care at all. Obviously, I answer that it's literature, that I find inspiration in real facts and I study them with passion and method. They don't believe me. They say it's too much for a writer knowing so much, as writers don't deal with this kind of power; as in their experience they have never seen an intellectual being acquainted with so much filth.[6] (2005a)

The letter, addressed to the 'Indian friends' – namely the blog readers, is structured around interrogatives and ends with an informal greeting formula:

> And I ask you, how much is it right to pay for one's piece of writing? What are the calibers defining it? Is there a measure? Is it right to undergo such a pressure? Does it grant the sense of success? I never end to pay for some sentences I have pronounced. And this denotes my narrative incapacity. . . . I get burnt. And the burn does not provide advantages to anyone. . . . When you write such things, instead, you play to be defeated, you stake a number which does not exist on the roulette wheel. But you do it the same. . . . *A close hug to you all. r.*[7] (2005a; my translation from Italian)

The second excerpt, instead, taken from 'Lettera alla mia terra'/ 'Letter to my land', written after the Castel Volturno massacre – one of the most cruel episodes of terrorism and violence causing the death of six innocent African migrants who were fiercely killed in September 2008 – is addressed to his fellow countrymen and was first published in *La Repubblica*. The cruelty of an ongoing violence, exerted on the only group of people who had tried to defend their dignity and right to work, results in Saviano's civil interrogation:

> I ask my country: what do we do now? Tell me. Should we just carry on? Pretend everything is normal? . . . How much longer do we have to wait? How much longer do we have to watch the best among us leave the country and see only the acquiescent remain? Are you certain that this is the way it should be? Are you certain that this is the evenings you spend courting, laughing, fighting, swearing at the smell of burning rubbish, or exchanging a few words are enough for you? All you want is a normal life, a life made of small things. Yet there is a war going on around you. How did we get so blind? So servile, resigned, bowed down? How is it that the Africans of Castel Volturno, the weakest of them all, who are violently taken advantage of by both the Italian clans and other African mafias, knew how to respond with more anger than fear? Personally I cannot believe that a South so rich in talents as ours can be content with the way things are. (Saviano 2012: 27–29)

To conclude, although engendered by the dysphoric attitude, and caused by deep indignation towards the world Saviano portrays, euphoria is an underlying means for hope, resistance, action and 'moralization', the last of the five phases analysed by Fontanilles in his canonical schema of passion, as the existence of a moral discourse assumes a pathemic dimension first (2001: 260).

THE SUBALTERN SOUTH: IS A POLITICS OF CHANGE POSSIBLE?

The pages of the article 'Letter to my land' are also some of the pages where Roberto Saviano reveals his most intimate connection with his homeland, and, at the same time, he provides a harsh representation of it. As we know, the idea of 'representation' – a key notion in cultural studies – refers to 'the process by which the members of a culture use language (broadly defined as any system which deploys signs, any signifying system) to produce meaning' (Hall 1997: 61). The representation of a culture, however, meant also as the image a culture has of itself and which communicates outside, can also be the 'site of possible change . . ., the place where battles are fought and strategies of resistance renegotiated' (Chow 1993: 29). Furthermore, following Hall, as things do not have in themselves any fixed, final or true meaning, but it is us in society, within human cultures, who make things mean (1997: 61); then images may 'provide alternative sights, alternative ways of watching that *would change the image*' (Chow 1993: 29). Particularly, according to Rey Chow,

> One of the most important enterprises nowadays is that of investigating the 'subjectivity' of the other-as-oppressed-victim. 'Subjectivity' becomes a way to change the defiled image, the stripped image, the image reduced to nakedness, by showing the truth behind/beneath/around it. The problem with the reinvention of subjectivity as such is that it tries to combat the politics of the image, a politics that is conducted on surfaces, by a politics of depths, hidden truths, and inner voices. (1993: 29)

The issue of the investigation of subjectivity and, above all, that of reinvention of subjectivity – both connected with the notion of representation – is central in 'Letter to my land', as we can read in the following excerpt. Here the subjectivity to be investigated is the south, which Saviano so frequently evokes saying 'my land'. In the following excerpt, the predominant terms – which in the Italian original are even more emphasized – are related to the semantic fields of 'see', 'represent', 'imagine', namely to the capacity of building new visions and scapes:[8]

> Here is a group of killers freely roaming around your land – our land – and massacring mainly innocent people. There are five or six of them, and they are always the same ones. How can this be? It makes me wonder: how does this country *see* itself? How does it *imagine* itself? How do you *think of* this country? [emphasis mine] How do you feel about yourself when you go to work, take a walk, make love? Do you ever bother to ask yourself or do you just say 'it has always been this way and it will always be this way?' Can you really believe that nothing depends on you, or on your want of indignation? Do you really think that worrying about your everyday life is enough? Are you satisfied by the answers to these questions? Does saying 'I'm not doing anything wrong; I'm an honest person', allow you to feel innocent? Can you let the news wash over you, over your soul? It has always been this way, hasn't it? Or maybe you hand over the task of making accusations to various organizations – the Church, militants, journalists and others? Does that make you feel better? Reassured enough to go to sleep at night? Perhaps not happy, but at least in peace with the world? Is that really enough for you? (Saviano 2009d: 20)

In this passage, as well as in most of his works, Saviano's reflections and considerations deal with the south, *his* south, and the still urgent and unsolved 'southern question'. For Saviano, the south is not a separate and distinct entity from the north, but a part of the intricate and wicked network of cultural, industrial and economic links with it. According to Gabriella Gribaudi,

> it may seem obvious that the idea and therefore the identity of the South of Italy (*Sud, Mezzogiorno, Meridione*) has been moulded through its dialogue with the North, yet the various works which have been published on this subject rarely take this factor into consideration. . . . North and South have interpreted each other through scientific paradigms and pre-existing stereotypes; they have exchanged images and representations, fashioning their respective identities by reflecting one another. . . . The South is much more than a geographical area. It is a metaphor which refers to an imaginary and mythical entity, associated with both hell and paradise: it is a place of the soul and an emblem of

> the evil which occurs everywhere, but which in Italy has been embodied in just one part of the nation's territory, becoming one of the myths on which the nation has been built. (1996: 73–74)[9]

As also Derobertis points out (Brunetti and Derobertis 2009: xix), Saviano shows the knots of this complex web, as well as the role of the South in it, focusing on the workings of the economy and trying to understand what economy leaves behind: dump, namely 'the most concrete emblem of every economic cycle' (Saviano 2008e: 282):

> Accumulating everything that ever was, dumps are the true aftermath of consumption, something more than the mark every product leaves on the surface of the earth. The South of Italy is the end of the line for the dregs of production, useless leftovers, and toxic waste. (282)
>
> The clans manage to drain all sorts of things from north to South. The bishop of Nola called the South of Italy as the illegal dumping ground for the rich industrialized north (287).
>
> The south is flooded with trash and it seems impossible to find a solution (295).

Saviano's personal cartography of the south also highlights accurate insights into the role of women in the physical and mental microcosm of *Gomorrah,* as well as into the subverted values of religion, family and honour. But the core of the southern question, coinciding with the tragic diaspora of 'southern brains' leaving Campania, Puglia, Calabria and Sicilia towards the north and foreign countries caused by the power of criminal mobs in the silence of politics and media, is clearly stated by Saviano in the following passage:

> Criminal mobs decide about everyone's destiny in this damned South, where one must choose between to emigrate and be lucky enough to find someone who could help you – a politician, a relative, a friend, a friend's friend – and take you on there. It is as if the land is split between the resigned people staying there and the ambitious ones going away. Not only hasn't the famous southern question . . . been solved yet, but it has not even been faced. There is a huge internal emigration. In these years millions of people have left from the South, also and above all because criminal mobs prevent their happiness. And preventing one's happiness means leading one to think of being powerless and

> not able to do anything that is not authorized by others. (Saviano 2010b: 46; my translation from Italian)[10]

Besides re-opening a front of debate on the southern question often silenced by media, *Gomorrah* and Saviano's whole work have also suggested a way to change the actual representation of the South and, hopefully, for the emergence of a new paradigm. By means of the analysis and 'tale' of the reasons for the south's ongoing crisis and widespread inability of modernization, new possibilities and solutions for Italian politics, society and culture may be envisioned. As Saviano states, 'Many will say and say again that what I do is sully the reputation of my country. And I will reiterate and reiterate again that this is the only damned way to try and change the state of things' (2010b: 28; my translation from Italian).[11]

So far in Italian history, particularly since the end of the Second World War, the representation of the south and the southern question has been classified into three main paradigms: the paradigm of dependence (representing the south as the victim of a systematic process of exploitation of resources and expropriation in favour of richer and stronger areas); the paradigm of modernization (interpreting the South as an area affected by a 'delay of modernity' where social, economic and cultural traits prevent the progress) and, finally, the paradigm of autonomy (Cassano 2009).

Particularly, this latter discusses the basic assumption of the southern question assuming the 'pathologic condition' of the South as the result of a cultural construction reinforcing a dominant image of the South built by stronger subjects. Moreover, as Cassano points out, the paradigm of autonomy suggests a new representation of the South as an independent entity able to rescue itself from any complex of inferiority and so to read and interpret critically crucial aspects of modernity (52).

In this sense, 'Letter to my land' can be arguably considered as Roberto Saviano's political, civil and literary manifesto: to observe reality, be indignant at its order of things, understand, resist and act jointly. As the author states,

> I cannot believe that only a few exceptional individuals fight back. Or that only priests, teachers, doctors, and a handful of honest politicians plus some groups that understand the role of the civil society, are prompted to expose the truth. What about everyone else? They sit quietly by, stunned by fear into silence.

> Fear. The biggest alibi of them all. Fear makes everyone feel safe. It governs your family, your affections, your own sacrosanct right to build your life and live. It would not be hard to stop being afraid. We just have to act, but together. (Saviano 2012: 31)

To use Gramsci's words, the southern question described by Saviano[12] can be considered as an 'organic crisis' involving politics in a much broader sense. Indeed, as Stuart Hall points out, Gramsci's concept of organic crisis includes the ' "trenches and fortifications" of civil society and the creation of a new level of "civilization", beside the questions of moral and intellectual leadership and the educative and formative role of the State' (Hall 1997).

In this sense, Saviano constantly attempts to create a new level of civilization informing and educating citizens by means of his all-media strategy. Moreover, as an organic intellectual who is a 'constructor, organizer, "permanent persuader" and not just a simple orator' (Gramsci quoted in Bowman 2008: 124), Saviano has sparked a renewed attention on mafia issues, especially in terms of audience quantity. By means of the active use of all mass media as the site of the possible cultural change and as instruments to spread a counter-hegemony, Roberto Saviano's words question the existence of a new cultural, political and economic paradigm, a new ideology, both in 'his land' and in Italy as a whole, encouraging people to become empowered through their knowledge, civil and political engagement.

To conclude, it is in this last excerpt from 'Letter to my land', and particularly in that 'first sign of freedom' wished for by Saviano, that one can trace the major task of cultural studies as the area of critical intervention and ethical-political project:

> I ask my country if it can imagine choosing. I ask if it is capable of exhibiting the first act of freedom: thinking you are different, that you are free. Not giving up and accepting what other men have created as your natural destiny. Those men can tear you away from your land and your past. They can take away your peace of mind. They can stop you from finding a home, scribble insults about you on the walls of your town. They can isolate you. But they cannot eradicate that which remains a certainty and which consequently is a hope: that is not fair or natural to keep down a region using violence and exploitation. Things cannot go on like this simply because they always have. . . . We need to find the strength to change. It is now or never. (Saviano 2012: 32–33)

META-JOURNALISM, OR THE CRITIQUE OF CRIMINAL IDEOLOGY

The representation of Saviano's homeland is also conveyed to the readers through the deceptive language of some major local newspapers, mainly sold in Campania: *Il Corriere di Caserta, la Gazzetta di Caserta* and *Cronache di Napoli*. On various occasions, such as in the Raitre TV show *Che tempo che fa*, Roberto Saviano has deconstructed the communication strategies used by these newspapers, financed by the camorra clans and read by many people of the region, to promote their ideology. Saviano's contribution, focused on the analysis of newspapers' headlines, titles, language and pictures, has been variously defined: a civil oration, a lesson on media, a theatre performance, a recital and an investigative report, all at the same time (Grasso in Saviano 2010b: xiv).

Some of the titles commented by Saviano are: 'Bin Laden and "O sceriffo" controlled business affairs' and 'Jovine's murder: 'O lupo and "nasone" in court'.[13] The readers' attention is immediately caught by the large use of nicknames (Bin Laden, 'O sceriffo, 'O lupo, nasone) to name the bosses. As Saviano states, 'Nearly every boss has a nick-name, an unequivocally unique, identifying feature. A nickname for a boss is like stigmata for a saint, the mark of membership in the System' (Saviano 2008e: 56). Nicknames, often ironic and deriving from old family names based on physical traits, or emerging suddenly out of somewhere, 'pump their bodies full of the power they hope to suture onto their skin' (222). Basically, nicknames avoid the pronunciation of the bosses' names, thus promoting the construction of a mythical halo around them. According to Saviano, besides, local newspapers use such labels as a linguistic strategy to create a sort of intimacy between the journalists who write the titles and the people who read them. This results in the spreading of obscure messages for people who do not live in those places and ignore the clans' national and international business affairs.

Other titles commented by Saviano are 'Giustiziato sindacalista' (2010b: 35)/ 'Trade unionist executed', and 'Pirolo, la corte assolve l'infame' (36)/ 'Pirolo, the villain acquitted by the jury'. In these cases, Saviano's focus is on the editorial choice of using the terms 'giustiziato' and 'infame'. As the writer explains, these words are strongly connoted. As a matter of fact, the term 'giustiziato' literally means that 'justice has been done', so it is a term presuming the existence of a legitimate form of power – which is not the state power but the criminal one – that can decide to do justice. The word 'infame', instead, is usually used by mafias to refer to justice informers, just like Pirolo, a justice informer acquitted for a crime (36–37).

In the same TV program, Roberto Saviano also highlights how some bosses manage to write from their jail cells and publish their letters on local newspapers, despite their 'hard prison regime' – the '41-bis' provision preventing any form of communication with the outside. Moreover, Saviano analyses a large amount of pictures, published by the same local newspapers, whose main protagonists are children assisting to murders in the streets or following the white coffins of their killed mates riding roaring motorbikes. As Saviano states, for these guys, the act of following these coffins using the motorbikes they received as a gift by the camorra in return of their employment as drug pushers seems to be the only worthy requiem.

It is clear then that the titles of these newspapers, as all news titles, convey underlying and implicit messages which exert the most important function in communication. As Calefato argues, they both build the ideological framework of a message and express its illocutive function, and they induce audiences to behave in a precise manner and adopt a precise hierarchy of values. For Calefato, news titles are a proper example of verbal signs that orientate audiences in understanding texts and even the words contained in the title (Calefato 2008: 75). For this reason, the frequent use of slanders ('Don Peppe Diana was a Camorrist'),[14] the semiotic construction of a boastful playboy image of the bosses ('re degli sciupafemmine'), the repeated use of pictures portraying young people seeing street murders, as well as the act of hosting the letters of inmate bosses in the news are only a few examples of an 'anaesthetic language' for the audiences' conscience. This kind of language makes people accustomed to the 'banality of evil', and to the passive acceptance of the existing order of things. As Saviano writes,

> Addiction [to this kind of language] becomes so strong that you end up reading and interpreting these facts as they are told you, without doubting on their genuineness. These titles, this kind of information constructs a world that it would be wrong to consider as a world of its own. It is the world of business, and it is the

> world of massacres. It is the world which invests money in Milan, in Parma, in Barcelona, in Berlin. But it has its roots in the South of Italy. (2010b: 36, my translation from Italian)[15]

Roberto Saviano has given other speeches using meta-journalism as a technique of analysis on various other occasions, such as in the Raitre TV programme *Vieni via con me* in 2010 and, more recently, in spring 2016, both in *Che tempo che fa* and in *TV-Talk*, another programme broadcast by Raitre. In the former programme, the object of his intervention was the deconstruction of the mechanism of the so-called macchina del fango. In the latter, instead, Saviano's aim was to deconstruct the messages of a much-discussed interview carried out by popular journalist Bruno Vespa to Salvo Riina – the son of the mafia boss Totò Riina – during the TV program *Porta a Porta*, broadcast by Raiuno, where Riina had been invited to launch his book.

Particularly, during *Vieni via con me*, Saviano denounced the existence of a danger for Italian democracy under Berlusconi's government, mainly caused by the crisis of press freedom. In the namesake book collecting the speeches he gave in that TV programme (2010b), Saviano explains that although in Italy nobody is put in jail for what he or she writes, some Italian journals use 'dossiers', sold to the readers as 'inchieste' or investigative reports, which are nothing else than defamatory reports. According to Saviano, this kind of 'macchina del fango' is typical of regimes, and it has also been used in the recent past, in Italy and abroad, against popular 'targets' like Pierpaolo Pasolini, Giovanni Falcone and Anna Politkovskaja, as well as against less famous anti-mafia victims. The 'macchina del fango' is characterized by dossiers, complicit journalists and politicians who try to delegitimize their adversaries using extortions and the media power, and to divert the audience's attention from inconvenient truths. Particularly, while investigative reports collect different elements to be shown to the readers, defamation uses a single element which has to do with private life – for example homosexuality, like in the cases of journalist Dino Boffo and political candidate Stefano Caldoro – and makes it public. This single, private, element hasn't usually got any connection with the public role of the 'target person' but forces him or her to defend himself or herself from despicable accusations (Saviano 2011b). According to Saviano, the mechanisms of the 'macchina del fango' were really dangerous in Italy under Berlusconi, as they were breaking the pact of confidence between the voters and the political class. The main objective of the 'macchina del fango', indeed, was to show the voters that they could not trust anyone, since everyone has his or her own faults and makes compromise to reach a political aim.

Finally, by means of the deconstruction of Bruno Vespa's interview to Riina broadcast by Raiuno on 7 April 2016, in the *TV-Talk* episode of 9 April 2016, Roberto Saviano denounces the risk of having emphasized the message sent by Riina to his desired addressees: some old 'Cosa Nostra' members, some new mafia affiliates, a part of the anti-mafia organizations and a part of the state. In the country, the public debate on this interview developed around two factions: some believed it was not right to transmit the interview, others reckoned it had to be broadcast trying to neutralize the messages the son of the boss wanted to convey. According to Saviano, this did not happen, due to the journalist's inability to catch and decode the real content of the interview, full of cryptic messages, which Saviano interprets as follows: the 'old mafia' – a term which is totally absent in Riina's speech – is disassociating from 'the new one'. Hence, despite still keeping their traditional 'values' that the 'new mafia' does not respect, the old mafia families declare their non-involvement in today's criminal affairs, and for this reason they ask for reductions in punishment without turning into justice informers.

A WRITER ON TV. *VIENI VIA CON ME*: A MEDIA EVENT

In an interview to the literary magazine *Stilos*, Roberto Saviano declared that for him television is fundamental: first, he owes the military protection to his media exposition; thus television protects him physically; but, more importantly, television is functional to his main objective: to disseminate his words to the largest number of people possible, and in this sense TV is an exceptional medium. As he states,

> I'm not as arrogant as many intellectuals who consider television as the 'devil's dirt' and, at the same time, I'm not so naïve to believe that it's enough to be accepted to change the television syntax. But I have found some spaces, for example Fabio Fazio's

> show, a space that allows me to reach a vast audience without compromising my message.[16] (Saviano 2010d: 19; my translation from Italian)

As a matter of fact, Roberto Saviano has had the possibility to take part in several TV shows after the publication of *Gomorrah*, but his first great television 'tests' have been the two special episodes of *Che tempo che fa* (2010), the Raitre show hosted by Fabio Fazio, titled 'La parola contro la camorra'. As it always happens for Saviano's media appearances, on television as well as in theatres, the scenic design is a minimalist one: a big crystal desk is surrounded in the background by the headlines and pictures of the most widespread newspapers of the area around Naples, which Saviano comments and deconstructs, as we have seen in the previous paragraph. The host, Fabio Fazio, accompanies the writer on the stage, sitting on Philippe Starck's famous 'Louis Ghost' chair, transparent itself. The presenter and writer's visibly moved faces, while receiving a standing ovation of the public who clapped at Saviano's 'television lecture', as well as the fixed gaze of the camera as a close-up on the writer's face, soon reveal a relevant detail: in this lecture the text is evidently important, but it is likewise important Saviano's presence and charisma on the stage: his body, pauses, obstinacy and emotions stifled with difficulty (Siti in Saviano 2010b: v).

Hence Roberto Saviano's two special episodes of *Che tempo che fa* – which gained an extraordinary audience success telling about stories of camorra, but also about literature – reopened the possibility to consider the return of the intellectual on the prime-time mainstream television scene, mainly dominated by inconsistent programs, such as reality shows. As Valentina De Carlo writes about the return of philosophers on TV in her introduction to *Videosofia* (2010) – a statement I will extend to intellectuals more in general – the philosopher's gestures, voice sounds and visibility reappear after centuries exactly thanks to tele-technology, or television. Aware or not of this, the philosopher on TV brings again the philosophical discourse out of the page, venturing himself in the realm of secondary oral transmission engendered by electronic media (29–30).

And yet, what happens when intellectuals appear on TV? What happens to their discourse when this is thrown away in the hypermarket of 'artifactuality'? The issue here is a Derridian one. Indeed, as Derrida puts it,

> Like many others, I think that one of the problems experienced, really by anyone who expresses himself in front of a camera, but particularly by intellectuals, teachers or writers, who are concerned to prepare or watch what they say or to proceed with caution, one of these problems which can turn into a political drama, is that they feel enjoined by a contradictory injunction: they must not refuse to bear witness or cut themselves off from the public sphere, which is dominated, today, by television in general, but at the same time they are less than they are in the position – I won't say to appropriate – but in any case to adapt the conditions of production, of recording, of what we're in the process of doing here and now, in such artificial conditions, to their own requirements. (Derrida and Stieger 2002: 32)

Saviano shows his awareness of how unreal is for a writer the fact of working for a TV programme, and of how the syntax of television is so peculiar. As he points out, everything you write on a page is a space for imagination, and everything you tell can be experienced, thought of and re-elaborated in the readers' head and soul. This is not the same on TV, where words are not written but must be seen. For Saviano, in a television narration, articles are the studio lights, adjectives are the clips, verbs are the scenery movements, sentences are the camera framings and finally guests are the punctuation. Everything must be included in a limited time, particularly the will to tell a meaningful slice of existence and the honesty to tell it as a point of view, not as the only, absolute, truth (2011b: 10).

Despite his feeling of unfamiliarity with the medium – which in this case is television, but which could be any other medium different from 'the page' he is accustomed to work with – Saviano acknowledges the challenge that the media throw at people working with words, namely the need to reconquer every time one's legitimacy to pronounce them. He writes:

> When I saw I had won the battle against reality shows, I realized that this had a meaning going beyond me, beyond what I said, beyond my face, beyond what I write. This meant that people want writers on TV. People want to listen to stories, they want different paths, different speech and discussion time, different ways to engage with arguments. (2010d: 19–20)[17]

This necessity to adjust the journalistic and literary speech to the rhythms and styles of TV was definitely embraced by the authors of the November 2010 television event: *Vieni via con me*, the Raitre prime-time show in four episodes, written and presented by Fabio Fazio and Roberto Saviano, and produced by Endemol. The reasons why this TV programme has been considered as a media 'event' are many. First, because it received a huge media coverage, both by means of traditional media and by means of social media; second, with reference to the social and political issues addressed (people's right to end-of-life decisions; eco-mafias; the responsibilities of the 'Commissione grandi rischi' in the 2009 earthquake at L'Aquila; the presence of 'Ndrangheta in the north of Italy) and the kind of guests invited (mainly ideologically opposed to Berlusconi's government); third for the audience results (on average, nine million people watched the programme during the four episodes, an unexpected datum, given the constant decline of viewers for the generalist TV channels). More importantly, however, *Vieni via con me* has been the first TV program in Italy to be consumed online and 'just in time' via social media, where users retweeted on Twitter (or shared on Facebook) contents and comments to the show, hence creating a virtual community, a sense of belonging and an innovative performative rituality (Andò and Comunello 2012: 92).

The main intent stated by Fazio and Saviano was to create a popular TV programme, to be able to reach the widest audiences possible, alternating narrations to entertainment, and to create 'an alternative place to what one can usually watch on TV' (Saviano 2011b: 11; my translation from Italian). With this intention, Saviano writes eight monologues, alternating to sections of music and theatre dance, and, above all, to lists ('elenchi'), the fundamental narrative structures of the show, emphasized by the soundtrack of 'Via con me' by Paolo Conte. The lists, which mainly concerned issues related to Italian contemporary culture, were read during the show by the presenters and their guests and also included lists sent by viewers via the web page of the programme while it was on air. Some of the issues were: the list of useful things to fight mafias, read by magistrate Piero Grasso; the list of words used to name homosexual people, read by gay politician Nichi Vendola; the list of things women can no longer stand, read by actress Laura Morante.[18]

In Patrizia Calefato's view, the enormous success of these 'lists' – a kind of language game reproduced in other contexts too, for example on the website of *La Repubblica* – is due to their immediacy. As a matter of fact, the choice of their constitutive terms is, at the same time, simple and well reasoned, as lists aim at defining an idea in a few traits, but they also open up to an 'encyclopaedia' of values, ideas about the world and memories, which are often more thorough than long and rambling speeches. Moreover, for Calefato, lists are a kind of writing whose constitutive signs anchor, or re-anchor themselves, to experience (2011: 24–25). Probably for this, in a crucial moment for Italy, when citizens were about to witness the slow end of Berlusconi's government and knew well they would endure its ideology still for long, Roberto Saviano commented on the sixty thousand 'lists of the reasons why life is worth living', collected on *La Repubblica* website, in this way:

> banal lists, the cynics will say; full of hypocrisy and mushy feelings, the wiseacres will say. But whoever is able to listen to words sincerely knows that it's them who are belittling and minimizing, being afraid of simplicity when it becomes a sense of life and, above all, an anchor for happiness. For, the search for happiness, as embodied in these lists, coincides with the necessity of a new beginning, a new country, a new horizon. (http://www.repubblica.it/spettacoli-e-cultura/2011/03/24/news/roberto_saviano-14025237/)[19]

The critiques to *Vieni via con me* arrive soon. According to Aldo Grasso, this TV programme is similar to a religious ceremony and a liturgical function. In his opinion, the lists are like litanies, and the viewers surrender to the appeal of a fervent supplication, to popular devotion and lamentation as their only source of hope and comfort (2010). Also for Alessandro Trocino, *Vieni via con me* is a laic prayer, whose rosary is made up of lists, the apical moment of surrender to Berlusconism. Particularly, for Trocino, the iterative structure of sentences and slogans in the show does not accomplish an informative and critical function, but just an emotional one (2011: 5–6).

Whatever are the more or less extremist positions in favour or against the intellectuals on TV, and particularly in favour or against Roberto Saviano's TV performances, it is evident that these programmes – often considered as mass TV rituals – have forced the reflection on several issues. First, these programmes have given television élite operators the possibility to think of new formats to inform the audiences on political and social affairs and to promote literature on a publicly broadcast prime-time popular TV show, mixing information and entertainment, where the physical presence of the intellectual on the scene is fundamental. Here, in fact, the body of intellectual can regain the oral tradition of narrations and tales. Second, *Vieni via con me* has suggested a reflection on the engaged communities and audiences – who are often very distant from TV consumption, but who have shown their interest in a strong social dimension of consumption helped by social media for the first time in Italy (Andò and Comunello 2012) – and on their interest in political and social issues. In this sense, an engaged community is, above all, a community able to participate emotionally in the life of a country and hence to modify its future course of actions. Indeed, as Saviano states,

> After every tale we felt the sensation that the audiences stopped being just audiences, and felt like citizens. No longer only viewers, each one isolated in one's own room, in a parterre or in front of one's computer. No longer bearing alone the discouragement of a sad story or the vital energy of a nice one. We felt the sensation that something was getting a move on, that there was the desire of understanding and acting, of being-in-the-things. We did not want to build a parallel reality; rather we wanted to narrate as in a Greek theatre where everything is part of the life of the *polis*, where there is participation, identification. . . . Tales do not have the ability to modify what has already happened, but they can modify what will happen. This is the greatness of narrations: when stories are heard, they become a part of those who feel like stories are their own stories and act on what has not yet happened. Every tale has this indeterminate margin, lying in the conscience of those who listen. Listening to a tale and feeling like it is one's own is like receiving a formula to repair the world. . . . a tale can become a contagious form that by transforming people transforms the world itself. (Saviano 2011b: 22–23; my translation from Italian).[20]

Finally, *Vieni via con me* has also been the chance to reason on a relevant part of the contemporary Italian cultural industry, and particularly on Rai, the public broadcasting service, as an 'industry of the imaginary'. As Saviano highlights, there have been many attempts of indirect censorship of the programme on the part of several Rai general managers, such as the granting of a small TV studio for the show; the attempt of reducing the number of episodes, limiting the number of guests and cutting their cachet off; the suspension of the programme manager Loris Mazzetti; the Rai reprimand letter sent to Raitre for a two-minute overrunning of the expected finishing time in the last episode of the programme and, finally, a strongly competitive show scheduling with other TV channels. According to Saviano, all these sly strategies aimed at limiting the audience share thus making the programme a niche show, contrarily to the ambitions of its authors and hosts who wanted to create a popular programme to be able to show some light beyond the 'night' of Italy (2011b: 10–11).

However, despite the programme was finally on air in autumn 2010, it is evident now that mainstream Italian public television was not ready to welcome quality products for the mass culture. The media can be emancipatory and transformative tools for the people and precious tools for intellectual and critical interventions, as well as for the mediation of political-cultural projects with very different types of audience. But Rai quit the challenge. The following programme by Roberto Saviano and Fabio Fazio, written along the lines of *Vieni via con me* and titled *Quello che (non) ho*, was broadcast by La7, a private TV channel. Roberto Saviano's latest TV appearances, instead, mainly addressed to a public made up of young people, went on air on Canale 5, during the show *Amici* (2015), and on Canale Nove (formerly DJTV), in a solo show titled *Imagine* (2015), both private broadcasting companies.

THE VIRUS OF INTERSEMIOTIC TRANSLATIONS: RADIO AND THEATRE

Roberto Saviano's process of media experimentations started in November 2006, some months after the publication of *Gomorrah*, when he took part into a Radiotre show entitled *Il Terzo Anello. Ad alta voce*. Here, with his voice accompanied by a soundtrack, Saviano tells the stories of a wider narration titled *Napoli. Dentro il vulcano*, made up of ten episodes lasting about half an hour each. The stories concern the major systems of Italian economy seen from the viewpoint of Naples and its inhabitants: the illegal drug market at Secondigliano (a suburb in the north of Naples), the route of cement in the construction industry; the role of women – the managers and victims of camorra – ; dumps, and children's life at Scampia (another suburb in the north of Naples). While narrating these tales, Saviano offers suggestions on the power of writing in exerting influence on real life and devotes the last episode of the programme entirely to literature. Differently from what usually happens during this radio programme, Saviano does not *read* his tales, but he *narrates* them. The style is his typical one, clear and informative, and the tales leave the space to the author for some stock phrases, interjections and other discursive signs, which are not necessarily functional to the narration, but even so useful to make the storytelling nearer to the actual features of oral speech. This definitely assumes and, at the same time, determines a closer contact between the narrator and the listeners.

An interesting topic faced in the radio programme is that of rap and hip hop music groups, like the Co' Sang, the 'A67, and the Kosanost, born in the Naples suburbs of Marianella, Scampia and Secondigliano. Particularly, for Saviano, rap musicians, who started producing their music after the so-called 'faida di Secondigliano' (2004–2005)[21], have become the most authentic voices in those territories as they live in first person the experiences they sing, they clarify what the camorra is in very simple terms and in some cases they embody a kind of negation of rappers' ethics. For instance, in the refrain of their song 'La camorra song io' (I am the camorra), the 'A67 explain that the camorra cannot be restricted to the alleys of Naples's historical centre, but it permeates people's mind and mentality, their way of thinking and acting, which forbids them to win the fear of denouncing the criminal power:

> 'A camorra simm nuje
> ca tenimmo paura 'e parlà
> e ci guardà dinto pe' ascì
> 'a chesta mentalità.

According to Saviano, the music production of these groups is now one of the best forms of writing in the south of Italy for it deals with the everyday life of young people living on the borders of criminality without expressing moralistic judgements on them and, meanwhile, without exalting them, like, on the contrary, neomelodic music does, as we will see in the next paragraph.

As for the theatre, Saviano declared that the idea that *Gomorrah* might be transposed into a play seemed part of its destiny even before the publication of the book (2012: 54). The idea, indeed, sprang from the collaboration between Roberto Saviano, Mario Gelardi (a young director) and Ivan Castiglione for the Teatro Mercadante of

Naples. The performances took place in Naples and in other Italian theatres between 2008 and 2009 and involved a group of young actors and non-actors 'who wanted to challenge themselves and gain an entirely new experience of the theatre', distant from its 'traditional paths and sacred cows' (55). After being interrupted for two years, the performances started again in 2011, putting on the scene five stories taken from the non-fiction novel *Gomorrah* and one dealing with the relationship between Saviano and his stories, characters and life 'after *Gomorrah*'. As Gelardi explains, he wanted to write a play totally independent from the book, but which did not betray its typically picturesque atmospheres; moreover, Gelardi's intention was to depict Roberto Saviano differently from how the collective imaginary often does, portraying him either a hero or a sly guy.[22]

February 2010, instead, was the time of Saviano's theatre debut as a protagonist, no longer as a character interpreted by an actor, in a play titled *La Bellezza e l'Inferno* (Beauty and The Inferno). Though this work has nothing to do with an intersemiotic translation of *Gomorrah*, it is nevertheless valuable to highlight Saviano's conception of the theatre as a form of disseminations of ideas and values. The play in question was directed by Serena Sinigallia and characterized by a minimalist scenery, made up of a retro wooden chair and a maxi screen where some pictures and videos useful to the narration are projected. On the armoured stage – guarded by the 'carabinieri' of the protection group – of the 'Piccolo Teatro Grassi' in Milan, Roberto Saviano narrates the stories of some people who have used their talent to defeat 'the Inferno' and search for the 'truth'.

But what is to be meant by 'beauty', 'inferno' and 'truth' in Saviano's perspective? The writer gives his definition of 'beauty' and 'inferno' in the opening essay of the namesake book, *La Bellezza e l'Inferno* (2009c), an anthology of articles written between 2004 and 2009. As he puts it, the title has a very simple meaning: 'It reminds us, on the one hand, of the freedoms and the beauty that are vital for the living writer, and on the other hand of their opposite, their negation: the hell that seems to have become the norm' (2012: 15). The inspiration for these ideas, continues Saviano, derives from *L'homme révolté* by Albert Camus who once wrote:

> for us who have been thrown into hell, mysterious melodies and the torturing images of a vanquished beauty will always bring us, in the midst of crime and folly, the echo of that harmonious

> insurrection which bears witness, throughout the centuries, to the greatness of humanity. . . . hell can endure for only a limited period and life will begin again one day. (Camus quoted in Saviano 2012: 15–16)

Another article, titled 'Truth, despite all else, exists', clarifies Saviano's conception of truth, his obsession:

> Truth obsesses me more than anything else. It is the *idée fixe* behind my book. Truth is not measurable: parameters, proofs, results of research never actually reveal the truth, but they can get close to it, they can circumscribe it. What ends up getting measured is the possibility of actually articulating the truth, its spaces, its perimeter, the conditions it needs for it to be generated. We can understand the time is spent on research and reflection, or the path that might lead to a truth. We can argue about it, struggle to find a way of saying it. Above all, we can find the instruments that will help us focus on it; find a perspective that does not just simplify what is complex but allows it to become visible and legible. Yes, because the truth – any kind of truth – needs first and foremost to be read. (2012: 56)

Saviano's monologue in the play starts with the narration of Neda and Taraneh's stories, the two young Iranian women killed by militiamen while they were protesting in Teheran streets against the vote riggings of 2009 presidential elections, and who became the symbols of the revolt against Ahmadinejad's regime. Then, shouldering a true AK-47 rifle, Saviano uses the figure of the Russian general Kalashnikov, the inventor of that weapon of mass destruction, to denounce the role of Italy as the second producer of weapons in the world. The performance continues with the narration of Alfred Nobel's (hi)story, the inventor of dynamite who chose to finance the Nobel Prize with his revenues, as a sign of repentance for what he had created. To inform and captivate the variegated public of the 'Piccolo Theatre' of Milan, Roberto Saviano does not use any special effects, except his words. His narrations shine a light on many other interesting (hi)stories, such as that of Miriam Makeba, the voice of the south Africans against the apartheid; of the journalist Anna Politkovskaja, defamed and killed for denouncing the question of Chechnya; of Varlam Shalamov, a writer who survived the cruelties of the gulags. All these tales have contributed to define Saviano's theatre performances as an example of 'civic theatre', a genre quite in vogue in those years in Italy, which the writer comments as follows:

> I like to see the word 'civic' next to the word 'theatre'. In my view it is good to put opposites together, not only because that adds to a project and reveals new artistic dimensions, but because it helps to fill a gap. Beyond theatre and art, nobody investigates or tells stories about the tragedies of the world. No mapmakers of possible happiness. No-one to echo the howls of pain. No-one to take the time to tell stories, to name the guilty, to chronicle events or compile a bibliography of witnesses – but when these empty spaces have been filled by theatre and literature, they reveal the enormous gaps that were once there. . . . The paradox is that theatre – the locus *par excellence* of lies and fictional representations – becomes a place of possible truth. And consequently, of truths. (2012: 55–56)

One cannot say that Saviano is a proper 'civic actor', and one cannot even say he can use drama techniques, like moving his body correctly on the stage or modulating his voice by means of correct respiration and articulation of sounds. Nevertheless, he does not even demand this, as from the very beginning of his play he defines himself as an 'abusivo del teatro'. And yet, performing himself and highlighting conflicts and contradictions, he has been able to take advantage of the theatre as a different space from the pages and other mass media to inform the public on issues that are rarely discussed somewhere else. In theatres you can explore new directions, because the theatre 'allows us to look each other in the face, to hear words bounce off one another, to sniff each other out' (2012: 56–57). And when you look at him while moving on the stage, permanently on the border of the stage itself, it seems that he is exactly trying to establish a contact with those people, his audience, to defend his truths.[23]

CINEMA AND TV-SERIES

The cinematic adaptation of *Gomorrah* took place in 2008, directed by Matteo Garrone, a film *auteur* considered as a part of the new wave of Italian cinema, able to regain centrality and appeal to wide audiences. The film, indeed, received great audience success as well as numerous relevant prizes and special mentions, in Italy and abroad, such as the Oscar of Italian cinema, or Davide di Donatello, the Grand Prix at the 61st Cannes Film Festival, the European Film Awards, and a nomination for the USA Golden Globes. The film *Gomorrah,* which is set during the period of the 'Faida' and is almost entirely shot in the most crumbling suburbs of Naples and Caserta (particularly in the housing blocks known as 'Vele di Scampia' or *Sails of Scampia*), selects some independent episodes from the book and joins them together using the different manifestations of the violence, cruelty and criminality of camorra as its central common narrative thread.

As Saviano explains, the film and the book complement each other without overlapping: they are autonomous creations in a specular relationship. In the film the camorra is a form of life and death of the everyday; it is neither a monster nor an aberration (2008a). Nevertheless, in many cases, the filmic transposition of *Gomorrah* enhances the narrative effect of the *non-fiction* novel, penetrating the world narrated by the writer even more deeply thanks to the exceptional medium of the Neapolitan language. This may not be true for the English-speaking audience, as the English subtitles in both the film and its DVD version have not prevented the problems of the target audience's understanding of the source text and its linguistic and social structure, so in many cases their watching experience may result impoverished. As Flavia Cavaliere (2010) accurately shows in her study on the subtitles and translation strategies at work in the English version of *Gomorrah,* in this film

> Non-Italian audiences who are unfamiliar with the sounds and rhythms of standard Italian are not even made aware that the characters are making extensive use of dialect, since in the film Neapolitan is always rendered in standard English. . . . English subtitles mainly resort to inclusive language, that is language which does not represent people on the basis of gender, place of birth, age, social status or other factors, and consequently important social and cultural markers such as class-related accents and ethnic or geographical dialects are totally neutralized. Audiences must infer such details from visual clues and from reading the subtitles with reference to the voices that utter the source text; subtitles are not read in isolation. Nonetheless, much can be lost in the double translation from written text to film subtitle and from dialect to standard English. . . . English subtitles do not

> convey any of the characters' uneducated and grammatically limited parlance, even though '[d]ialectal usage, swearing, deviant grammar or even inarticulacy help set the context of culture, and both dubbing and subtitling techniques should be called upon to provide some clues'. (180–181)

And yet, as it has been happening in Italian cinema since the beginning of the 2000s, the dialect in *Gomorrah* is employed with both aesthetic and realistic aims: its main task is to highlight the social marginality and delinquency of the film characters, besides expressing their mere geographical collocation (De Ruggieri 2008). The absolute 'impression of reality' is guaranteed to *Gomorrah* by a number of factors: first, the actors, who in some case were taken from 'the street'; second by the predominance of dialogues; and third by the film costumes. The latter, despite being almost imperceptibly spectacularized, function as the supporting element of the 'aller-rétour' relation (Metz quoted in Calefato 2008), according to which 'reality enters the world of cinema, it is filtered and transformed by cinema, and always brings with it a bit of cinema when going out from it', as Calefato suggests (148; my translation from Italian). With regards to this, it is noteworthy to mention how the classic gangster cinema has permeated the reality portrayed in the film (and novel) *Gomorrah*. Longing for their belonging to the criminal word, the young inhabitants of Naples's slums spectacularize their life turning to the classic imaginary of gangster films to build their identities and roles within the interpersonal relationships they build in their territory. Hence in *Gomorrah*, book and film, the linguistic and cultural conscience of the most represented social group is essentially grounded in filmic representations, which constitute 'a sort of "modelling principle" of social conscience' (Calefato 2008: 143; my translation from Italian).

The myths of cinema loved and imitated by the young and old men and women of the System include *Scarface* by De Palma, *Donnie Brasco* by Mike Newell, *Il Camorrista* by Tornatore, as well as *Kill Bill* by Quentin Tarantino and *Nikita* by Luc Besson. As Saviano puts it, for the people of the System, cinema is a treasure trove to be sacked in order to build a proper criminal image and appearance. Moreover, the cinematographic imaginary permeates so much the reality of the suburbs described by *Gomorrah* that one can listen to phrases and sentences taken from the aforementioned films while walking across the streets of Naples's slums (2006b; D'Orrico 2011).

In the book *Gomorrah* Saviano had already highlighted how every crucial moment in the life of a boss is perceived as the scene of a spectacle or performance. For instance, it is the case of the capture of the boss Cosimo Di Lauro, who evidently inspired himself to Brandon Lee in *The Crow*, which Saviano describes as follows:

> When Cosimo hears the pounding of boots and the clatter of rifles, he doesn't try to escape. He doesn't even arm himself. Instead he goes to the mirror, wets his comb, pulls his hair off his forehead, and ties it in a ponytail at his nape, letting the curly mane fall onto his neck. He is wearing a dark polo-neck sweater and a black raincoat. . . . The new military sovereigns of the Neapolitan criminal associations don't present themselves as neighborhood tough guys. . . . *The Matrix*, *The Crow*, and *Pulp Fiction* give a better idea of what they want and who they are. They are models everyone recognizes and that don't need too much mediation. Spectacle is superior to enigmatic codes of winking or the well-defined mythology of infamous crime neighborhoods. Cosimo looks straight at the camera, lowers his chin, and sticks out his forehead. . . . Cosimo has been brought up in the world of show business, and he knows how to go onstage. (2008e: 110–111)

Hence it is not the world of cinema that scans and peers at the protagonists of the criminal world, but the opposite is true: for Saviano, 'Movies are the source for forms of expression' (see the chapter 'Hollywood' in *Gomorrah*; English trans: 244–258). Therefore, in *Gomorrah* – book and film – the semiotic practice of citation, defined as 'a practice of recombination and a prototype of intertextuality', as well as a 'decontextualizing discourse practice' (Dagostino and Calefato 2007, my translation from Italian), makes evident the mechanism by which it creates an estranging effect. The practice of citation in the film *Gomorrah* works, first and foremost, at its first level, namely the reported speech. This is particularly obvious in a fragment of the story of Marco and Ciro, the two brash teenager protagonists of one of the narrative strands of the film. The two guys, who desperately long and struggle for their own place in the criminal world, are fascinated by the myth of Tony Montana in the film *Scarface*, a role played by Al Pacino, and in a scene where they are the protagonists they reproduce a dialog taken from that film. They have learnt by heart the most relevant lines, as if this was an exercise aimed at learning the sentences, postures, sayings or, in other words, the *part* they want to play in their life. For, as Saviano states, 'it's not true that films are a lie, that you can't live as in the movies, that as soon as you stick your head out of the theatre, you realize things are not the same' (2008e: 256). Thus, every cited film owns its 'extraterritoriality', as Dagostino would say; once you use the citation in a different context, it stops being a copy and turns into an original. Moreover, in the act of citation, this copy circulates getting rid of its source (2006): from cinema to reality, then, from the screenplay to life. All this gives the sense of how cinema, if interpreted from a socio-semiotic perspective, is evidently a 'social technology' and a 'social practice', a place creating and nourishing the collective imaginary. In this sense, cinema is not only an apparatus of visual reproduction but also a system entangled in the production of meanings, values, ideologies and subjectivities (De Ruggieri 2008).

In this process of construction of the collective imaginary, a crucial part is also played by the cinematic sound and music. Particularly, as for the soundtrack of *Gomorrah,* most of it is made up of neomelodic music, a style created in Naples, which since the late 1970s has been considered as the soundtrack of 'illegitimate Naples' with its slums, camorra, drug traffic, hidden economy and war among the competing criminal clans. As Saviano once put it, neomelodic singers are often *camorristi*'s friends and singers of the camorra ideology (2008a), and in the film *Gomorrah,* Garrone uses neomelodic music to emphasize what Roberto Saviano narrates in this excerpt:

> their MP3 player with the music they listened to when they went to do pieces . . . was now dangling from [Pikachu's] neck. . . . I immediately stuck the headphones in my ears; I wanted to know what trawler background music was. I was expecting rap, acid rock, heavy metal, but instead it was an endless round of Neapolitan neo-melodic music and pop. In America, killers pump themselves up on rap, but in Secondigliano they go off to kill with love songs in their ears. (2008e: 109)

It is known that music is considered as a semi-symbolic system – a notion introduced by Greimasian semiotics – which establishes a correlation of interdependence between the expression values and the content values. This correlation varies from text to text, making their signs not isolated symbols. Particularly, in the realm of the film discourse, music guarantees meaning production essentially in its correlation with images and pictures. As De Ruggieri points out, in film discourse music *cinematographises* itself when it meets pictures, so as to become evocative of a film sequence or of the film as a whole. Music and pictures are in constant dialog with each other throughout the film, and thanks to this relationship they modify and contaminate each other (2008: 43–44).

In the film *Gomorrah* the neomelodic music has a vivid and representative function: besides highlighting the situations where this genre or style is mostly listened to in the territories portrayed from the very beginning of the film, it also emphasizes the so-called napoletaneria, thus contributing to define the film atmospheres. With reference to the cultural phenomena produced in Naples by the feud of Scampia, Marcello Ravveduto (2007) counterposes exactly the idea of 'napoletaneria' with that of 'napoletanità' or *Neapolitanness*:

> If 'napoletanità' is a collective play which has made the people of this city so seemingly European, and yet so truly southerners, with their wit and acumen, a rare sense of humour, a (nostalgic and melancholic) irony and a will-to-be vocation which makes them so unquiet and restless, 'napoletaneria' is the degeneration of the common feeling, it transforms the play into an acting with an end in itself. 'Napoletanità' is an aching wound, a grief which generates culture: the city tells the world its disadvantage, it communicates a universal image of marginality by means of its dialect. 'Napoletaneria', instead, is a form of demeaning exhibitionism. (82; my translation from Italian)[24]

'Napoletaneria', which has many degrees of pleasantness but also many undermost levels, distinguishes the popular culture of the state districts of Naples's slums and is the result of the homogeneous culture of these districts, whose inhabitants do not care about integrating their own artistic forms and languages with the other social classes of the city. In this way, as Ravveduto suggests, every district marks a social and cultural island detached from the rest of the town which is lived only as a way out for the consumption of local music production. Here neomelodic singers, who do not disdain the protection of the clans governing the district and who are content with their 'divismo', are the true defenders of a homogeneous culture which degenerates into 'napoletaneria' (83–85).

The multiple structural differences between the book and the film adaptation include the absence from the film of the narrative persona that represented a pole of positive identification for the readers. Although it is true that the film portrays some rare moments of tenderness and 'beauty' – such as the case of children playing in the small rubber swimming pool on the *Sails'* roof; the old lady trying to bring some order in her piece of countryside devastated by toxic waste disposal; and the character of Roberto, the young technical assistant working for the stakeholder company of toxic waste who decides, at some point, to stop working in that field, thus showing a possibility to resist – these moments are defined by Saviano himself as 'voluntary dystonias in a damned cycle of events' (2008b, my translation from Italian).

Nevertheless, the real attempt to envision the possibility for the spectators to – at least – resist the fascination exerted by the criminal world, if not that of interposing a clear distance between us and that nasty reality, is probably provided by Garrone, Saviano and their fellow scriptwriters's choice of the film genre. As a matter of fact, *Gomorrah* clearly stands in the tradition of Italian neorealism with its real locations as sets and ordinary people as characters, and is by far different from the Hollywood's model of mafia movies that Italian and foreign audiences are accustomed to watch. As I wrote earlier, in *Gomorrah* there are several references to American classic gangster movies, but Garrone's deliberate aim was that of going 'in the opposite way of that model' (Mottram 2008). Garrone tries to demythologize the criminal clans and their supposed heroes, making them seem ridiculous and pathetic while they try eagerly to imitate the Hollywood gangsters. It is widely known that Hollywood mafia films glorify the criminal lifestyle, glamorize their dons and romanticize about them by showing their strict adherence to codes of honour, rules of conduct and loyalty to family ties. However, as Cavaliere points out, 'Hollywood can glamorize gangsters because in the celluloid world justice will always finally triumph and social order will always be restored, but in the world of *Gomorrah* there is no such thing as punishment for crime and the social order no longer seems to exist' (2010: 176).

Hence, the main subject matter of the film *Gomorrah* is a very dark reality, where almost no space is left for the 'good'. This is exactly the same subject matter of *Gomorrah – The Series*, Roberto Saviano's latest but not the least relevant and successful idea for an intersemiotic translation of his book, even more emphasized by the absolute predominance of gloomy atmospheres of the setting with most of its scenes shot at night.

Similarly to a contemporary Shakespearean *Macbeth*, written from the sole perspective of evil, this new work of transmediation of the film *Gomorrah* aims at representing a universal reality starting from the criminal dynamics occurring in Naples and its peripheries. Hence, the main themes of this series are the thirst for money and power, the portrayal of evil in its multifaceted nature with the conflicts it engenders, the consequences it provokes, the reactions it arouses and the means it uses to penetrate the human soul and behaviours. Although the two seasons of the series are a deliberate work of fiction – revolving around the Savastano crime family, their wicked affiliates, cruel rivals and their relationships with the wider local and global world of criminality, business and politics – most of the dialogues are based on real wiretappings and in the plots it is not difficult to trace the worst workings of our time, in whatever town, city or country we are happened to live. As Saviano states,

> I didn't mean to chew the dinner before the tablemate chocked. I want the risk of choking to exist, of feeling reality deeply, and I hope that once we come into this reality, everything around us may change, that people may have the possibility to study and look at reality with 'more dioptres', to quote Francesco Rosi. (2015a)[25]

Perhaps this is the reason why *Gomorrah – The Series*, made up of twelve episodes in each of the two seasons[26] and broadcast simultaneously in Italy by the pay-TV channels Sky Atlantic and Sky Cinema 1 in 2014 and 2016, respectively, has been reckoned as the most successful Italian TV programme in history. Sold in more than one hundred countries all over the world, it has reached success in the USA and in the rest of the world and has been compared to other recent cult TV series. Particularly, *Gomorrah – The Series* has been defined as 'a darker, grown-up version of 'The Sopranos', or as 'The Wire: Italy', as both series 'provide unflinching insight into worlds most viewers are afraid to acknowledge (even when they're already surrounding us)' (Travers 2016).

As it is typical of the genre of TV series, from a narrative point of view *Gomorrah – The Series* (from now on referred to as *Gomorrah – S*) provides a double storyline: one that ends in each individual episode, and another that runs through the whole season and even beyond it. This is one of the ways to assign continuity to a series, so *Gomorrah – S* might be ideally broadcast forever as long as the viewers and the ratings show interest in it. It is known that TV series lack any definite closure, but what really makes them appealing for the audience is the occurrence of cliffhangers, namely the narrative devices aimed at ending the story in great suspense to interest the viewer in the next instalment or season. In the first season of *Gomorrah – S*, for instance, the main cliffhanger involves the character of Genny Savastano, suspended between life and death. As for the characters, of course their personality traits develop throughout the single episodes and seasons; moreover some of them remain central, other totally disappear, like in the case of Donna Imma, a female character dominating the first season. What is more, the authors and scriptwriters of *Gomorrah – S* show interest in portraying how the categories of race and ethnicity as well as those of sex, gender and sexuality determine the characters's features, actions and representations. For instance, the representation of migrants in season 1 is particularly evident in episode four, titled 'Sangue africano', where the dynamics of power and revenge between a local group of Africans – addressed as 'monkeys' – and the boss Savastano are manifest. In season 2, instead, women are some of the protagonists: particularly, they are shown in their growing authority of strong, independent, successful and assertive characters (see the character of Scianel for example, who perfectly replaces that of Donna Imma in season 1), while homosexuality is portrayed by means of the character of Salvatore Conte.

Another fundamental aspect which *Gomorrah – S* shares with all other TV series is the rituality of collective participations of its fans who take part into the process of viewing and consumption with a very critical approach. On social networks, blogs and particularly on dedicated Internet discussion groups, the fan communities analyse and comment on episodes in detail, argue in favour of or against certain future developments or try to orientate specific storyline developments or the reappearance of their favourite characters. This is the case of the character of Salvatore Conte, who will probably be on the screen again in the third series, after the big pressure of the fans' community on the authors of the series.

Similarly to what happened around the book and its author, also *Gomorrah – S* has been at the centre of controversies in Italy, especially for the accusation of defaming Naples and its people, and for the supposed empathy that the characters raise in the viewers, thus increasing the desire of emulation, particularly on the part of the weakest young spectators. However, apart from the two factions pro and con this argument, what is interesting to highlight here is an unusual, ironic and fun reaction to these critiques, which also stands as an example of the user-generated contents the web often encourages creatively. I refer to the work of the collective of Neapolitan videomakers, 'the Jackal', who have produced a parody of the TV series which has soon gone viral, called 'Gli effetti di Gomorra La Serie sulla gente' (The effects of *Gomorrah The Series* on people). The four short films – which in episode 2 also star the actor Salvatore Esposito playing the role of Genny Savastano in the series, and in episode 3 star Roberto Saviano in the role of himself[27] – play on some language expressions and attitudes of the characters distinguishing certain topical scenes of the series. The Jackal's work provides a brilliant deconstruction and caricaturization of the language, characters and situations which in the series look so hateful, disgusting and dreadful, and at the same time contribute to soften the polemics around the series.

Finally, the theme song of *Gomorrah – S* deserves a mention, particularly the final one which starts with the sounds of 'Doomed to life' by the Mokadelic' – the soundtrack of some of the most crucial moments of the series – and then softens until blending with a Neapolitan rap/hip-hop song by 'Nto and Lucariello. The song is titled 'Nuje vulimme 'na speranza', in Italian 'We want *a* hope', and its lyric deals with young people's hopes for the future in the desolate waste land of Naples, wider metaphor for the contemporary world. Theme songs have been defined as some of the main ingredients and peculiar traits of TV series, which impress upon the collective imaginary and stand like thresholds between the ordinary world and the world of the 'pleasuredome' of fiction (Attimonelli 2010). It is significant that the opposite happens in *Gomorrah – S*: a subtle sense of pleasure and catharsis affects the spectators while they listen to the words of the final theme song. On the threshold between the horrors of the fictionalized truths and the truths of ordinary reality, the theme song functions as a suspended time for the spectators, who enjoy the pleasure of *hope* in the sole space in the series where this word can be used. 'Pleasuredome' can only lie in this interstice.

NOTES

1. Recently Roberto Saviano has declared on his Facebook page that he is currently working with Tel Aviv–based illustrator Asaf Hanuka on a graphic novel concerning his life, due out in Italy in November 2017 and internationally shortly thereafter. The book, represented by the Andrew Wylie Agency, is being developed and edited by BAO Publishing in Italy.

2. Italian original version: 'lo scrivere, come esperienza del linguaggio in quanto linguaggio, si mostra così come corrispondere, continuamente, assiduamente, senza alcuna garanzia di giungere a destinazione, senza nessun percorso e nome assicurati, ma non per questo senza tensione, senza ostinazione, sempre in circolazione, continuamente rilanciato'.

3. Since the death of journalist Giorgio Bocca, Roberto Saviano has continued the news column titled 'L'Antitaliano' on the weekly magazine *L'Espresso*.

4. Italian original: 'la passione . . . non è riducibile alla sola manifestazione linguistica di superficie o agli usi lessicali. Certamente la presenza di lessemi passionali che si riferiscono direttamente a una certa emozione, come pure un'alta ridondanza di aggettivi e avverbi, le categorie lessicali che più marcatamente veicolano qualificazioni emotive, sono indicatori di un discorso appassionato, ma molti altri sono i livelli che possono contribuire a creare un effetto patemico, come il ritmo della narrazione di un evento, o la descrizione di un volto, di un'espressione, di un comportamento'.

5. Italian original: 'La cosa che genera scandalo è che uno scrittore, il mestiere considerato più innocuo e incapace di poter avere alcun tipo di forza sulla realtà, possa d'improvviso divenire responsabile di una luce che prima era sbiadita e sbilenca, di uno sguardo infame che spiffera ciò che si vuole celato, che urla quello che è sussurrato, che traduce in sintassi e insuffla vita a quello che prima era disperso in frasi frammentarie di cronaca e sentenze giudiziarie. La vita o la si vive o la si scrive, diceva Pirandello, eppure ci sono momenti in cui la vita la si scrive per mutarla. Ciò che mi è capitato in questi giorni ha generato apprensione e scandalo, ma in realtà non per quello che è accaduto – dalle mie parti ciò che mi è accaduto capita a moltissime persone, quotidianamente e per molto meno – ma perché è accaduto a uno scrittore. Per uno scrittore il modo per innestarsi nel reale è raccontarlo. È uno scrittore che può congetturare, immaginare ciò che non vede. La sua immaginazione e la sua congettura però non seguono l'arbitrio della licenza poetica, ma sono strumenti necessari per avvicinarsi ancora più al vero in ciò che osserva: oltre ai nomi, ai documenti, alle sentenze, alle intercettazioni. . . . Quando racconti un processo, quando raccogli la cronaca nera, quando ascolti le intercettazioni comprendi che l'unico modo per capire è raccontare tutto questo come parte di un corpo che nasconde i suoi organi. E d'improvviso quello che nel perimetro di certe zone conoscevano tutti, passandosi le storie di bocca in bocca, impastandole di particolarità soggettive e leggende, quello che finiva negli articoli di cronaca, quello che sembrava essere territorio di addetti ai lavori, operatori sociali invisibili ed esperti sociologi dell'antimafia, diviene il racconto di un intero paese, l'epica fascinosa e terribile di un capitalismo vincente che vede nel cemento, nei trasporti, nel tessile, nei subappalti, nei rifiuti, nella distribuzione e in quant'altro possa creare respiro al profitto, il proprio sterminato territorio di conquista'.

6. Italian original: 'mi chiedono che se proprio devo denunciare allora devo farlo formalmente. . . . Rischiando insomma, smettendo di scrivere, divenendo

elemento del processo non più osservatore. In breve rendendomi parte di una questione, quando con la scrittura mi ostino a mantenermi su posizioni altre, descrivendo l'intero meccanismo e non la singola questione. Affrontando dinamiche di potere non singoli crimini, di cui sovente non mi importa nulla. Io ovviamente dico che è letteratura, che mi ispiro a fatti reali e che li studio con passione e metodo. Loro non ci credono. Dicono che è troppo per uno scrittore sapere così tanto, che gli scrittori non si occupano di questi poteri, che loro che hanno esperienza non hanno mai visto un intellettuale conoscere tante "*schifezze*" '.

7. Italian original: 'E vi chiedo, quanto è giusto pagare per un proprio scritto? Quali sono i calibri che lo definiscono? V'è una misura? È giusto subire questo tipo di pressioni? Concede il senso del successo? Io spesso per alcune frasi non smetto mai di pagare. E questo denota la mia incapacità narrativa. Non ho la giusta misura, l'attenzione per l'equilibrio. Mi brucio. E l'ustione non dona vantaggio a nessuno. . . . Quando scrivi certe cose invece, giochi ad esser sconfitto, punti su un numero che non esiste nella ruota del roulette. Ma lo fai lo stesso. . . . Un abbraccio a tutti. Stretto. r.'.

8. Italian original: 'E io mi chiedo: nella *vostra* terra, nella *nostra* terra sono ormai mesi e mesi che un manipolo di killer si aggira indisturbato massacrando soprattutto persone innocenti. Cinque, sei persone, sempre le stesse. Com'è possibile? Mi chiedo: ma questa terra *come* si *vede, come si rappresenta a se stessa, come si immagina*? *Come ve la immaginate voi la vostra terra, il vostro paese*? Come vi sentite quando andate al lavoro, passeggiate, fate l'amore? Vi ponete il problema, o vi basta dire, 'così è sempre stato e sempre sarà così'? *Davvero vi basta credere che nulla di ciò che accade dipende dal vostro impegno o dalla vostra indignazione?* . . . Vi basta dire 'non faccio niente di male, sono una persona onestà per farvi sentire innocenti? Lasciarvi passare le notizie sulla pelle e sull'anima. Tanto è sempre stato così, o no? O delegare ad associazioni, chiesa, militanti, giornalisti e altri il compito di denunciare vi rende tranquilli? Di una tranquillità che vi fa andare a letto magari non felici ma in pace? Vi basta veramente? . . . Chiedo di nuovo alla mia terra che *immagine* abbia di sé. Lo chiedo anche a tutte quelle associazioni di donne e uomini che in grande silenzio qui lavorano e si impegnano. A quei pochi politici che riescono a rimanere credibili, che resistono alle tentazioni della collusione o della rinuncia a combattere il potere dei clan. A tutti coloro che fanno bene il loro lavoro, a tutti coloro che cercano di vivere onestamente, come in qualsiasi altra parte del mondo. A tutte queste persone. Che sono sempre di più, ma sono sempre più sole. Come vi *immaginate* questa terra? (Saviano 2009c: 20).

9. In her article 'Images of the South', Gabriella Grimaudi argues that it was during the late nineteenth century that the theoretical construction of Italian dualism and a form of 'positivist racism' originated: the South was portrayed in photographs circulating around the country as 'a paradise inhabited by devils': 'a happy land, kissed by the gods, favoured by the climate and the fruitfulness of the soil', yet characterized by violence, anarchy, rebellions, endemic corruption, as well as by poverty and ignorance, which were actually the reasons for all these social problems.

10. Italian Original: 'i poteri criminali . . . decidono del destino di tutti, in questo dannato Sud, dove la scelta è tra emigrare o avere la fortuna di trovare qualcuno che ti aiuti – politico, parente, amico, amico di amici – e che ti possa sistemare. È come se il territorio si spaccasse tra i rassegnati che restano e gli

ambiziosi che vanno via. La famosa "questione meridionale" – parola che fa inorridire i più – non solo non è stata ancora risolta, ma non è stata nemmeno adeguatamente affrontata. Esiste di nuovo un'emigrazione interna enorme. Milioni di persone, in questi ultimi anni sono andati via dal Sud, anche e soprattutto perché i poteri criminali sono un ostacolo alla loro felicità. . . . E togliere la felicità significa proprio indurre le persone a pensare di essere impotenti, di non poter fare nulla che non passi per l'avallo o mani altrui'.

11. Italian original: 'Molti diranno e ripeteranno che ciò che faccio significa infangare il Paese. E io ogni volta ribadirò che invece questo è l'unico, dannatissimo modo per cercare di cambiare le cose'.

12. See also some of Saviano's most recent interventions on the South, particularly a speech on the political class governing Campania in the TV programme 'Servizio Pubblico' (1 June 2015); a letter to Italian prime minister Matteo Renzi http://www.repubblica.it/politica/2015/08/01/news/caro_premier_il_sud_sta_morendo_se_ne_vanno_tutti_persino_le_mafie-120219278/ (1 August 2015); an article on the necessity of a 'Southern revolution': http://www.robertosaviano.com/la-paranza-dei-bambini-nella-guerra-di-napoli/ (8 September 2015), and finally an article on the Democratic Party in Campania http://www.repubblica.it/politica/2016/04/28/news/la_politica_della_resa-138616723/ (28 April 2016).

13. Italian original: 'Bin Laden e 'o sceriffo controllavano gli affari'; 'Delitto Jovine: 'o lupo e "nasone" in tribunale'.

14. Don Peppino Diana was a crusading priest who denounced the camorra from his pulpit in Casal di Principe, organized protest marches and set up community programmes to siphon support for the camorra. As Saviano writes, Don Peppino Diana 'decided to take an interest in the dynamics of power and not merely its corollary suffering. . . . He didn't want merely to clean the wound but to understand the mechanisms of the metastasis, to prevent the cancer from spreading, to block the source of whatever was turning his home into a gold mine of capital with an abundance of cadavers' (2008e: 221).

15. Italian original: 'L'assuefazione diventa tale che i fatti finisci per leggerli e valutarli così come ti vengono raccontati senza dubitare della loro genuinità. Questi titoli, questo tipo di informazioni, costruiscono un mondo che sarebbe un errore considerare un mondo a parte. È il mondo degli affari, ed è il mondo dei massacri. È il mondo che investe a Milano, che investe a Parma, che investe a Barcellona, che investe a Berlino. Ma ha la sua radice nel Sud Italia'.

16. Italian original: 'Non ho la spocchia che hanno molti intellettuali di considerare la televisione come "sterco del demonio" e allo stesso tempo non ho l'ingenuità di credere che basta che ti accettino per poter cambiare la sintassi televisiva. Però ho trovato degli spazi, per esempio il programma di Fabio Fazio è uno di questi. Uno spazio che ti permette di arrivare ad un pubblico enorme senza dover compromettere il tuo messaggio'.

17. Italian original: 'Quando ho visto che ho battuto i reality mi son detto che tutto ciò ha un significato che va oltre me, va oltre quello che ho detto, oltre la mia faccia, oltre quello che scrivo e cioè che la gente vuole gli scrittori in televisione. Le persone vogliono ascoltare storie, vogliono percorsi diversi, tempi diversi di parlato e di discussione, modi diversi di relazionarsi'.

18. This is an example of a list read during the show: '1. Avere paura di uscire quando cala il buio; 2. Avere paura di uscire con il cane quando fuori non c'è nessuno; 3. avere paura di un marito geloso; 4. essere picchiata da un marito geloso; 5. essere uccisa da un marito geloso; 6. non poter indossare un abito corto sui

mezzi pubblici, 7. essere molestata in metropolitana; 8. sentir dire che si è state molestate perché si indossava un abito corto; 9. essere licenziata perché si vuole avere un figlio; 10. non trovare lavoro perché si è brutte; 11. non trovare lavoro perché si è troppo giovani; 12. non trovare lavoro perché si è troppo vecchie; 13. avere paura di non essere più accettata perché arrivano le rughe sul viso; 14. essere presa in giro perché si piange davanti a un film; 15. essere stuprata, molestata, insultata; 16. vedere le donne rappresentate costantemente come veline o come escort; 17. essere considerata intelligente, quindi pericolosa; 18. essere considerata bella, quindi stupida'.

19. Italian original: 'elenchi banali, diranno i cinici, pieni di ipocrisia e di falso buonismo, diranno i saccenti. Ma chiunque abbia ascolto sincero delle parole sa che sono loro a banalizzare, impauriti dalla semplicità quando diviene senso della vita e soprattutto punto fermo di felicità. Perché la ricerca della felicità, che si fa corpo in questi elenchi, coincide anche con la necessità di un nuovo inizio, di un nuovo paese, di un nuovo orizzonte'.

20. Italian original: 'A ogni racconto avevamo la sensazione che il pubblico smettesse di essere pubblico e si sentisse cittadino. Non più solo spettatori, ciascuno isolato nella propria stanza, in platea o davanti al computer. Non più portando con sé, da soli, lo sconforto di una storia triste o l'energia vitale di una bella storia. Avevamo la sensazione che si muovesse, che ci fosse voglia di capire e di agire, di essere nelle cose. Non volevamo costruire una realtà parallela, ma raccontare, come in un teatro greco, dove tutto è parte della vita della *polis*, dove c'è partecipazione, immedesimazione . . . Il racconto non ha la capacità di modificare quello che è successo, può però trasformare ciò che verrà. È questa la forza della narrazione: quando viene ascoltata, diviene parte di chi la sente propria e agirà quindi su ciò che non è ancora accaduto. Ogni racconto ha questo margine di indeterminato, che risiede nella coscienza di chi ascolta. Ascoltare un racconto e sentirlo proprio è come ricevere una formula per aggiustare il mondo. . . . un racconto può divenire una forma contagiosa che trasformando le persone trasforma il mondo stesso'.

21. This feud started with the fierce opposition between the Di Lauro's clan and the so-called Scissionisti. This real war of camorra, fought for the dominion on the territory and illegal affairs in the north of Naples, provoked the death of more than eighty people in two weeks.

22. See: http://www.teatrostabilenapoli.it/Archivio/produzioni/gomorra.

23. Finally, Roberto Saviano's latest performance is titled *Sanghenapule* (Naples blood). It is a play Saviano has defined as an act of love for his city, which was on the scene of the 'Piccolo Teatro Grassi' of Milan in April 2016. The play starts from the legendary figure of San Gennaro, the patron saint of Naples, and from the miracle of what is claimed to be his blood kept in a sealed glass ampule which every year, on 19 September, melts. The story, however, is a journey full of pathos within the inner nature of Naples and its inhabitants by means of an atheist focus on a whirlwind of imaginary, true, tragic and grotesque stories. In the play, two characters alternate on the stage, Roberto Saviano and Neapolitan playwright and actor Mimmo Borrelli. Particularly, Saviano plays the role of the narrator of the events and characters performed theatrically by Borrelli, who uses a powerful language and a magnificent performance of the body to interpret the mythical and real characters evoked by Saviano. Simultaneously, the play alternates two codes: mimesis and exegesis, rites and historical and political argumentation, thus creating a correspondence between

form and content as it also mirrors the incredible contradictions of Naples, a much-beloved and hated land for both authors (Giovannelli 2016).

24. Italian original: 'se la 'napoletanità' è una *recita collettiva* che ha reso il popolo di questa città così apparentemente europeo, ma anche così realmente meridionale, con una finezza di spirito, con un raro senso dello humour e dell'ironia (nostalgica e malinconica), con una vocazione al voler essere che lo rende così inquieto ed irrequieto, la "napoletaneria" è la degenerazione del sentire collettivo, trasforma la *recita* in rappresentazione fine a se stessa. La "napoletanità" è una lacerazione dolente, una ferita che produce cultura: la città parla al mondo del suo disagio, comunica un'immagine universale di marginalità attraverso l'uso del dialetto. La "napoletaneria" è, invece, una forma di esibizionismo degradante'.

25. Italian original: 'Non ho voluto premasticare la cena prima che il commensale si strozzi. Io voglio che ci sia il rischio di strozzarsi, di sentire troppo la realtà, e spero che una volta entrati in questa realtà, tutto intorno cambi, che si possa avere la possibilità di approfondire, di guardare la realtà con – citando Francesco Rosi – "diottrie maggiori" '.

26. Since October 2016, Season 3 has started to be shot.

27. See episode 2 on https://www.youtube.com/watch?v=QvLsS9fZuDg and episode 3 on https://www.youtube.com/watch?v=1PV5byp25yk).

FIVE

People have the power

Oltregomorra and the network society

OLTREGOMORRA: A CYBERTEXT IN THE WIDER REALM OF WORLD PROTESTS

The day Roberto Saviano was assigned police protection after the death threats he received from the camorra was 16 October 2006, and 16 October 2006 was also the date when many initiatives in support of the writer began to arise, especially out of the cyberspace. I like defining the whole of these initiatives as 'BeyondGomorrah', 'OltreGomorra' in Italian. Particularly, I refer to the opening of several websites showing solidarity with the writer; to the initiatives arisen from the social networks MySpace and Facebook; to *Gomorrah*'s choral readings in schools and squares; to school projects like the social advertising 'Una foto per Saviano' commissioned by the province of Caserta, and the street art project 'Savianocontinua' in Milan. Moreover, I make reference to the honorary citizenship conferred to Saviano by many towns; to the plea signed by many Nobel Prize winners and the thousand citizens' online petitions in his support. In short, I refer to everything that has revolved around Roberto Saviano as an icon since the publication of his first book, as well as to what has been intended to deconstruct his mythical and heroic figure. *Oltregomorra,* however, is first and foremost the name of one of the most relevant initiatives born on the Internet in those years; more precisely, it is the natural development of Roberto

Saviano's MySpace group into a website, www.oltregomorra.it, opened in June 2008 by a group of volunteers coordinated by Alessandro Pecoraro, a young student from Caserta. Pecoraro worked as the manager of Roberto Saviano's web communication, including the writer's first official website and the MySpace and Facebook pages, from 2007 to 2010. Then, the 'phenomenon Saviano' became unmanageable for a student of political communication working almost for nothing for 'Roberto', whom in the meantime had become his friend. Having knowledge of the development of the private/public events in Roberto Saviano's life and Alessandro Pecoraro's commitment in creating a virtual and real territory beyond the book *Gomorrah* can be interesting to understand how the ideas of 'impegno', citizenship and politics have changed in the age of social networks. Therefore, it is my intention to highlight shortly the most relevant steps of this development. Alessandro Pecoraro met Roberto Saviano during one of the first book launches of *Gomorrah* in a Caserta bookshop, and as soon as he learned of the protection assigned to the writer, he planned and carried out a series of initiatives in his support. Particularly, in a sole day, he created the website www.sosteniamosaviano.org (no longer available now), he wrote a letter addressed to the writer, to the president of Italian Republic and the presidents of 'Camera' and 'Senato', and finally he started a web petition in support of Saviano. The petition in solidarity with the writer went viral, and a number of TV stations like the BBC and CNN as well as French and Dutch newspapers contacted Pecoraro; later on, also the online version of Italian newspaper *La Repubblica* gave visibility to the website created by Pecoraro. Roberto Saviano's gratitude towards Pecoraro was made public on the last page of the book *Beauty and the Inferno* where the writer also pays homage to all the people who believed in him, stood by him and took part in his story in different ways:

> To Alex Pecoraro and those on the web who have built a network of information and solidarity. To those who used social networking sites like Facebook and MySpace to create a network of support and to generate publicity. (2009c; English translation: 274)

In 2007 Pecoraro collaborated with Saviano for the editing of the first version of his official website (www.robertosaviano.it, no longer available now), but his will to take advantage of all positive energy to create something positive and to offer many people the possibility to show concrete solidarity to Roberto went further on the web. In March 2008 he created the MySpace page of Oltregomorra which, as Pecoraro reveals[1], was mainly visited by female users aged around thirty, with a good cultural background. As this MySpace page grew, Pecoraro started a new cooperative project creating the website of Oltregomorra. According to the authors of this website, Saviano's literary work had been an essential and crucial starting point, but their aim was to work together questioning and thinking on the contemporary world and different sides of mafia ideology in order to 'go beyond, to make sprouts become deep roots' (http://www.oltregomorra.it/progettooltregomorra/; my translation from Italian). By using an Internet space always *in fieri*, Oltregomorra pointed at giving the audience 'a view on mafias different from the one outlined by traditional media' (ibid.). Precisely, all the website sections aimed at creating a databank on mafias and promoting the way of thinking and acting of 'Italy that resists', namely the whole of associations and institutions at work to deconstruct the several expressions of mafias ideology day by day. One of the sections constituting the website is an accurate 'Vocabolario della camorra', coordinated by Alessandro Pecoraro. As the author of the project maintains, this is perhaps the section that best embodies the goals of the website, since it aims at analysing common words (such as coffee, water, anorexia) which are here deprived of their original meaning and shown in their connection with the camorra. In this way, the dictionary reveals the mechanisms of camorra's infiltration within the state, its economy and culture, thus sharpening the readers' critical citizenship. In 2008, the year of Facebook boom in Italy, Alessandro Pecoraro created Saviano's personal Facebook page, reaching quickly the limit of five thousand 'friends' and, as a consequence, it had to be changed into a 'fanpage', counting more than two million four hundred thousand fans today. Nowadays, Alessandro Pecoraro's latest commitments for the promotion of an Oltregomorra space include the fostering of school projects on the theme of legality across Italy, and, above all, the co-foundation of Caracò Editore, a cultural association and publishing house devoted to social issues.

What comes out from this story is the key role of the digital public sphere as a starting point and a means for spreading information, creating empathy, generating social action – as single individuals first and as a community later – and consequently for transforming citizens' world view. This is evidently crucial, given the power of people's way of thinking in determining the fate of norms and values on which societies are constructed (Castells 2007: 238). In the case of *Gomorrah*, the social networks MySpace and Facebook, together with citizens' several online activities in favour of Roberto Saviano, 'created a community where virtuality was the most immediate prelude to the actual initiatives carried out in the squares' (Saviano 2008d). Therefore, the use of 'self-mass communication' (Castells 2007), and specifically of Internet, blogs and social networks, was the prelude to people's active and democratic participation in the process of deconstruction of mafia ideology.

Inasmuch the Oltregomorra space was born and developed essentially through the horizontal networks of interactive communication, before the initiatives planned in the cyberspace could become real, it is possible to define it as a cybertext. As defined by Patrizia Calefato (2011), cybertexts are electronic texts allowing us to accomplish an action not only by clicking with a mouse on them or brushing up against them with a touchscreen, but also to act socially (41). We can certainly say that Oltregomorra has acted socially contributing not only to foster people's knowledge and awareness on mafias, but also to promote a renewed sense of community in Italy in those years. The premise to this kind of social action is an idea of the political, shared by the web users who are also flesh and blood people, which Roland Barthes would define as 'the whole of human relations, in their real, social structure, in their power of making the world' (1994: 223). Similarly, the premise to this ideal of the political is also the belief that people can use their 'counter-power' to resist and challenge well-entrenched power dynamics and change the current state of things. However, to make this change, it is necessary to carry out relevant actions in the everyday life, which are the result of people's individual responsibility. Indeed, the existent social order depends on the actions that people reproduce daily, or, conversely, they manage to disrupt daily as men, women, workers, consumers and voters. Moreover, this idea of the political is based on the faith in common action and on a new-old idea of community and participation. As Saviano puts it:

> Now I know, thanks to the thousand citizens' signatures, . . . that something mine has become ours. After this experience a country

> is no longer a geographical entity, but my country is the whole of women and men who have decided to resist, change and participate, doing what one can do to the best of one's ability. (Saviano 2008d; my translation from Italian)[2]

Therefore, for Saviano the key imperatives of a concrete fight for greater awareness, social responsibility and change of the current order of things lie in common everyday life actions and active hope. As is evident, this is far from the rhetoric of heroic deeds of resistance, extreme sacrifice and idealistic struggle against evil, crime and 'inferno', ascribed to him by his detractors, as we have seen in chapter 1 of this book.

One of the most widespread slogans used during the manifestations of solidarity with the writer was 'Siamo tutti Saviano' (We are all Saviano), a slogan which was also the name of a Facebook page providing information for all the people who wanted to manifest their support to the writer, online and in the streets. The language structure of this motto is commonly used in several manifestations of protests, virtual and real, like in the case of 'We are all Khaled Said', the young Egyptian activist beaten and killed by the police of his country in an Alexandria cybercafé in 2010 after distributing a video denouncing the police corruption. Also in this case, the same motto gave the name to the Facebook page gathering all the people manifesting for freedom from Mubarak's regime in Egyptian squares. The peculiarity of these slogans lies in the idea of 'fusion' with the 'hero' in question, specifically the 'writer-hero' in the case of Roberto Saviano, and the 'young activist-hero' in the case of Khaled Said. This fusion is not simply an apparent linguistic and rhetoric strategy leading to a fake identification with the principal protester; on the contrary, it has a specific aim: to endorse the reasons for protesting and support the commitment of the people who have started or given new light to the protests. Although it might be true that claiming to protest is not necessarily to protest for a part of the fans of these Facebook pages, this could be the beginning of something productive and new in terms of identities, relations, practices, conditions and possibilities. To say it in Saviano's terms, this could be generative of 'the dream of something' ('il sogno di una cosa'), levering on a kind of technomagic bond between an 'idol' and a 'tribe' (first electronic, and later real). This bond stands as a new social pact 'where emotion, affects and shared symbols become the new matrixes of being together, the new assumptions of every collective fusion, confusion and effusion'[3] (Susca 2011: 80; my translation from Italian).

As we have seen, BeyondGomorrah is an example of how the fundamental values of the civil society in the age of information and networks – primarily those of citizenship and of the defense of freedom and rights – as well as the value of sociality are more and more immanent and articulated within the 'social-technical movements'. As Ned Rossiter argues, these movements are 'emergent institutional forms of organized networks' (2006: 13) permitting people to rethink democracy in the information society exactly in terms of 'organized networks' of communication, namely 'informal social movements' and 'virtual organizations'. These kinds of networks may be able to condition new institutions that are attentive to problems of scale and can address specific needs, desires and interests at different levels (supra-national, national, transnational, sub-national and intraregional). In addition, these new institutional forms are different from the modern ones (like governments, unions and firms) as their organization is grounded on verticality and representative principles of liberal democracies, and yet they are still 'institutional' for their ability to organize social relations. Indeed, according to Rossiter, nowadays it is within this digital terrain that people face, or organize to face, the issues concerning the cultural, social, political and economic life of a community. As Rossiter suggests, in this way civil society

> does not entirely disappear or become destroyed with the onset of neoliberalism from around the 1970s – '80s. Rather, there has been a maintenance of civil society within our current network societies precisely because there has been a social desire and need to do so. (73)

The crucial role of organized networks has been particularly evident and striking during the waves of protests and uprisings characterizing both a part of the Arab world and of the European and American West some years ago. Obviously, all the movements of protest arose for different reasons born of the local cultural and socio-political contexts, and of course led to different consequences. For instance, Teheran Twitter Revolution (2009–2010) was a protest movement against the irregular presidential elections of

Ahmadinejad and his government, whereas the protesters of the so-called Arab Spring (started in Tunisia in 2010) mainly fought against the violence of local regimes. The movement of Spanish 'Indignados' (started on 15 May 2011), instead, as well as the protests in Greece and New York 'Occupy Wall Street' in 2011, sprang as a reaction against the way governments managed the economic and financial crisis. The common aspect of these revolts, however, was people's sense of indignation and disgust for their governments (both totalitarian and pseudo-democratic, in the protesters' view), for the political class and for the connivance between the financial élite with the political one. But thanks to the novelties introduced by the cyberspace and particularly by social networks, with regard to people's feeling of being-in-common and to the process of coordination and amplification of protest movements, people's indignation overcame fear and turned into a large sensation of hope and desire of active participation aimed at political and civic transformations (Castells 2012).

In conclusion, organizing networks in the network society can be definitely considered as a way to achieve the new utopia lying at the heart of this new culture, which for Castells is the utopia of the autonomy of the subject *vis-à-vis* the institutions of the society. In fact, when societies are unable to manage the structural crisis of existing institutions, change can only happen outside the system by means of the transformation of power relationships starting in people's mind and growing in the networks built by the new actors of the history to come (190). And if utopias are not mere fantasies because they become a material force once they enter people's mind inspiring their dreams, guiding their actions and provoking reactions, then it is desirable BeyondGomorrah has been also the right way to start the path towards the utopia of defeating camorra and mafias, which is definitely Roberto Saviano's ultimate goal.

ITALIAN WINDS OF UPHEAVALS AND CHANGE BEYOND *GOMORRAH*

In the light of the wave of protests affecting Italy in the years following the publication of Roberto Saviano's first book, the BeyondGomorrah movement can be conceived as a paradigmatic case showing the germs of a widespread exhaustion for Italian cultural climate and of people's renewed sense of empowerment fostered by the increasing influence of social networks. Indeed, I believe the book *Gomorrah* and the deriving network of support to the writer marked a real watershed in Italian culture. The issues Roberto Saviano faced in his book and in the public events he took part into were regarded as urgent questions to be tackled and solved in the country. At that time, Italy was wrecked by near-economic default, immorality in the management of public affairs, destroyed authority of institutions, media domination, servile journalism, racist attitudes within institutions, infamous representations of women in the media, gender and class divide. Moreover, other problems which seem to affect the country constantly and eternally were particularly felt by the population: corruption, organized crime, unemployment and consequent massive emigration of graduate students towards foreign countries.

As a matter of fact, after 2006 Italy was coming to grips with *Berlusconismo*, which many perceived as the end of an era, and was facing a complete decline and a deep cultural and political crisis, as also portrayed by Annalisa Piras's independent documentary film *Girlfriend in a Coma* (2012). However, before Silvio Berlusconi's resignation, which took place on 12 November 2011 under pressure from the European Central Bank and among the whistles and celebrations of his opponents in Rome, the Italians had already shown to be tired of that thick veil of overall filthy stagnation. The desire of change, of rebirth and of a cultural revolution had already been evident thanks to the many protests reaching media attention. As I am going to show, some of them were strictly political – and precisely anti-Berlusconi – others were political and cultural in a broader sense. Let me outline shortly the profile of some of these upheavals and movements.

8 September 2007 in Bologne was the 'Vaffanculo Day' or V-Day ('Fuck off Day'), organized to carry out a citizens' petition concerning the Members of Parliament's election criteria. The organizer of V-Day was Beppe Grillo, the famous comedian leader (or spokesperson, as he preferred to be called) of the Five Star Movement (5SM) founded later on in 2009. Born as an anti-Berlusconi's protest organization, the 5SM soon became an anti-establishment political and activist web-based movement with a number of populist connotations. The movement was going to receive electoral success with more than 25 per cent of votes in the 2013 Italian national election, thus becoming the most voted party advocating a radical change in

Italian politics by means of fomenting people's political and social anger and economic despair using a vulgar language and violent tones. In October-December 2008, instead, another spontaneous movement of protest against Berlusconi's government emerged. Its name was L'Onda (The Wave) and aimed at denouncing the university and research cuts ordered by Berlusconi's Ministry of Education. Other protests recalling, in a sense, some of the first demonstrations of dissent against Berlusconi and people's disagreement with his way of conceiving politics and culture – the so-called *girotondi*[4] (human chains) – were the two No Berlusconi Days, or No B Days, organized, respectively, in December 2009 and October 2010. Both took place in Rome and simultaneously in many other Italian cities and world capitals including London, Berlin, Paris, Madrid, New York and Sydney. However, differently from *girotondi*, the two No Berlusconi Days lacked any specific political connotation as they were planned by bloggers and Facebook users to ask for Berlusconi's resignations. Within a short time, this protest evolved into a social movement organization, known as 'Popolo Viola' (Purple People), using different Facebook pages – all reaching huge immediate consensus among the users – to keep the protesters' community informed and united. This social movement mainly originated as a reaction against the so-called *lodo Alfano* – a controversial reform proposed by Berlusconi's government aimed at granting immunity to the four highest political offices in Italy and seen by many as an attempt to escape the trials he was involved in (Coretti 2012: 14), but it later modified its identity. Particularly, Popolo Viola changed from being an explicitly anti-Berlusconi movement to a more hybrid nature, getting involved in anti-mafia issues, anti-corruption, antifascism and solidarity to labour and immigration (14), and finally reducing its popularity collapsing, in the end, under internal tensions.

February 2011, instead, was the month of two other major protests: in the aftermath of the *Rubygate*,[5] intellectuals, activists, politicians, jurists and trade unionists, together with members of the civil society, gathered in Milan PalaSharp to ask, again, for Berlusconi's immediate resignation. In this way, they responded to the appeal written in four languages by some intellectuals on behalf of all members of the cultural association Libertà e Giustizia.[6] No later than a week, on 13 February 2011, also women said 'basta!' with Berlusconi's repeated violations of women's dignity and almost a million people – women and men different for their age, profession, political and religious creed – marched across Rome and many other Italian and world cities within a rally taking the name *Se Non Ora Quando?* (SNOQ, 'If not now, when?'). Also in this case, the road to greater mass awareness on women's offensive and disrespectful representation in the media was mainly opened by an activist, Lorella Zanardo. Indeed, in 2009 Zanardo had authored a short documentary titled *Il corpo delle donne*,[7] watched online by more than five million people and rapidly gone viral. The documentary investigated the reasons why Italian women did not take to the streets to protest against the surreal way they were portrayed on TV. As Zanardo observed, women's bodies were 'inflated to ridiculous proportions, like those of circus freaks', and this denied the representation of a more complex and at the same time genuine idea of femininity due to the obsessive repetitions of fake bodies, 'vulgar image(s) with silicone lips, thighs, breasts'. What's more, this kind of women soft porn representations were broadcasted at every time of the day on very popular TV programmes even by RAI channels, the national public television. Zanardo's documentary, which also later became a book and a project for teaching media education in schools, also denounced how that kind of women portrayal simply 'goes along with men's every desire and gives up any possibility of being an equal "other" . . . reduced or [self-reduced] to a sexual object fighting the passing of time'. Additionally, Zanardo highlighted the ordinary employment of women in useless TV shows, forced in a mute and decorative frame with no competence to show. Even some of the most emancipated women, in strictly professional contexts, agreed on being represented as desirable objects, deprived of their authenticity and vulnerability of their face. All this was evidently typical of the videocracy regime in which Italy – the country where 80 per cent of people use television as the main, if not the only, information source – had been lost for thirty years, since the birth of 'televisione commerciale' or private broadcasting (see Gandini's documentary film *Videocracy*, 2009).

Finally, on 15 October 2011, the Occupy Movement reached the Italian shores with a few thousand people gathered in Rome to protest against economic imbalance, highly precarious work and the consequent reduced (or denied) employment rights and precarious life experienced above all by the 'precari/e della conoscenza', knowledge workers in the field of education, research and publishing.

Now, as Arditi maintains, insurgences and protests are 'political performatives', namely 'actions and statements that anticipate something to come as participants begin to experience – as they begin to live – what they are fighting for while they fight for it' (2012: 4). In his view, although being sometimes episodic and vanishing, street protests and insurgencies always leave a legacy and have 'a spectral afterlife that is anything but ethereal because it impregnates practices and institutions as much as ways of seeing and doing' (14). Particularly, in Arditi's opinion, the materiality of this afterlife is evident in many ways, not the least 'the cognitive shifts insurgencies generate' (14) and 'the cultural artifacts they leave behind' (15), such as photos, blogs and websites, but also interviews, media analyses, conferences and publications, which try to give meaning to the events.

So, it is probably too soon to say if all the insurgencies and protest movements discussed earlier started to reconfigure radically power dynamics and relations within Italian institutions, particularly within the government and in the media. Nevertheless, some requests coming from the community of protesters – specifically related to women, anti-mafia, and anti-corruption issues – have been answered in the following years by the Parliament and Matteo Renzi's government, at least from a merely formal point of view. For instance, in 2013 the Parliament elected a woman, Laura Boldrini, as the president of the Chamber of Deputies – being now the third woman to cover this role in the history of Italian Republic – and elected anti-mafia magistrate Pietro Grasso as the president of Senate. In 2014, instead, Prime Minister Matteo Renzi respected the so-called *quote rosa* (female quotas) when he nominated the ministers of his government; hence it was the first time Italy had had the same number of women and men in charge of ministers of the Republic. Moreover, Renzi's government established the 'Autorità Nazionale Anticorruzione' (Anti-Corruption National Authority), presided over by anti-camorra magistrate Raffaele Cantone, to monitor national public tenders where illegality and mafias infiltrations are often unmasked, as Saviano's public denunciations had made evident.

Additionally, if we look at the new ways to achieve the power, Matteo Renzi possibly managed to conquer the Italian political scene using incisive political communication strategies based on the ideas of radical change, 'newness' and 'accessibility' as a direct consequence of the previous years of upheavals. Particularly, Renzi presented himself as 'il rottamatore', the leader who gets rid of the old, corrupted and inept political class, thus managing to penetrate common sense rapidly. In this, he was helped by specific communication strategies that definitively sanctioned the absolute relevance of social networks also in contemporary Italian politics. With Renzi, social networks have been used both to launch political slogans with hashtags like #cambiaverso (change direction), #Italiariparte (Italy restarts) and #laSvoltabuona (the right turn) and to establish a direct relationship with the citizens by means of very frequent 'tweets', Facebook posts and the new format #Matteorisponde – a question time with his followers.

Moreover, if we assume that politicians embody and perform their power in relation to the complex symbolic functions of their bodies – from a semiotic and fashion theory perspective – then their bodies undergo a 'transmedial construction', which is both the result of single performances or intentional marketing techniques and the product of a collective work entirely originating in the media. This process involves politicians' gestures, body language and clothing signs (Giannone 2015: 3–4). In the case of Matteo Renzi, with some attitudes and common gestures he reiterates, careless of the institutional role he is supposed to play like the 'selfie' ritual, he seems to have abolished any 'auratic' distance between power and common people (Giannone 2015: 6). Finally, drawing on the rhetoric of 'youthfulness', Renzi displays his renewed image of 'the chief's body' adopting a 'normcore', 'casual' and 'unfinished' clothing style. This means that depending on the situation, like 'one of us', Renzi wears familiar clothing items (jeans, shirts, leather jacket or suit), and often presents himself wearing a white shirt – the key item of his vestimentary performance – without a jacket. As Giannone puts it, the implicit meaning here is that 'he had to take his jacket off in order to work, move and act more easily', but it could also signal that 'he has not had the time to put his jacket on' (6). This way of continuously 'shifting the borders between front-stage and backstage', as Giannone maintains, 'is a central feature characterizing new forms of embodying power in the age of media, in which all-intrusive cameras *de facto* abolish the limits between private and public spaces' (6).

Is this also a way to prove that the previous political and social season is definitely over? Possibly so, even if Renzi's defeat in early December 2016 Referendum to change Italian Constitution proves what Renzi did and how he did it was definitely not enough for the Italians. In this regard, Roberto Saviano's 'owling'[8] analysis published in 2014 on the magazine *L'Espresso* sounds prophetic. Indeed, in his weekly column *L'Antitaliano*, Saviano criticized Matteo Renzi's way of governing the difficult condition of Italy. He criticized his arrogant and inappropriately optimistic approach to the country's problems, mainly made up of 'announcements', which at times resembled Silvio Berlusconi's political style and clearly contrasted with most of people's life conditions and perspectives. As Saviano wrote,

> Renzi has promised a lot, but facts are not following words and this is triggering a short circuit between expectations and reality. Everybody knows reforming the country is a titanic enterprise. The problems are so many and the consent so necessary to be kept that Renzi runs a serious risk: instead of changing the course of things, he is simply managing the course of things taking very small steps, which look relevant only if compared with the Berlusconian past, but not relevant at all if related to the necessary changes.[9] (2014)

A MICROPOLITICS OF AFFECTS: ROBERTO SAVIANO ON THE NET

To resume the central theme of this chapter, so far it has been argued that social media have proved their ability to shape a new ideology and counter-power of the collective identities and communities built in cyberspace. Social media can contribute to shape the preferences, attitudes and perceptions of individual subjects, and for this reason the micropolitics at work in the technomagic realms also contributes to the formation of desire, beliefs and judgement in political and social subjects and communities.

Now it is right to ask what are the features and main traits of these new collective identities, and how they have influenced Roberto Saviano's relationship with his 'followers'. For Susca and De Kerckhove, the networks of techno-social subjectivities built on social media are able to engender a 'communicracy' manifesting itself as a 'postmodern liquid form of power moulded in every situation in which a community vibrates in unison in a state of communion, around communication' (2008: 3; my translation from Italian).

According to the scholars, behind these 'technomagic bonds', one can glimpse the 'erotic urge moving the bottom of social life, the burning desire of joining the Other in a holistic way' (3). For Hardt and Negri, instead, the people or 'multitude' of the age of social networks build affective relationships within an intricate process of biopolitical production. This is typical of the Society of Control, namely the society whose 'mechanisms of command become ever more "democratic", ever more immanent to the social fields, distributed throughout the bodies and brains of the citizens' (2000: 41). In the age of Facebook and Twitter (the major platforms of biopolitical production), together with all other social media, the productivity of bodies and the value of affect play a crucial political role. This is true both with regard to the exploitation of subjectivities and to their revolutionary potential. Indeed, in Hardt and Negri's opinion, these new subjectivities, produced by great industrial and financial powers – which in their turn generate needs, social relations, bodies and minds (2000: 32) – live in the 'beyond measure' realm, in 'virtuality', namely the 'set of powers to act (being, loving, transforming, creating) that reside in the multitude' (357).

In the following section of this work, I would like to point out the processes by means of which affective relationships have developed around the figure of Roberto Saviano in the 'virtual' world of Facebook, the platform where the writer has the largest community of 'fans'. Moreover, I would like to highlight the revolutionary potential of subjectivities constituting the 'biopolitic collective body' Hardt and Negri speak about. First, however, it is necessary to define the notion of 'affect' structuring and determining relationships within the virtual realm, as well as the term 'affective' when it is associated with the noun 'relationship'.

One of the scholars who theorized the notion of affect is Brian Massumi, who defines it as 'primary, nonconscious, subjective or presubjective, asignifying, unqualified'. In this, affect is different from emotion which is, in his opinion, 'derivative, conscious, qualified, and meaningful', a 'content' which can be assigned to an already-constituted subject (Massumi 2002). With reference to Massumi's theorization, Shaviro explains that

> emotion is affect captured by a subject, or tamed and reduced to the extent that it becomes commensurate with that subject.

> Subjects are overwhelmed and traversed by affect, but they have or possess their own emotions. (2010: 3)

According to Shaviro, in today's regime of neoliberal capitalism, we consider ourselves as subjects to the extent that we are autonomous economic units. For this kind of subject, 'emotions are resources to invest, in the hope of gaining as much return as possible' (3). Moreover, for Shaviro, what we mean by 'affective labour' is not affective at all, as it implies the 'sale of labour-power in the form of pre-defined and pre-packaged emotions.' (4). Nevertheless, behind emotion 'there is always a certain surplus of affect that 'escapes confinement' and 'remains unactualized, inseparable from but unassimilable to any particular, functionally anchored perspective'' (Massumi quoted by Shaviro 2010: 5). Therefore, our life is always linked to an affective and aesthetic flow eluding cognitive definition or capture (Shaviro 2010: 4), and for Massumi 'it is precisely by means of such affective flows that the subject is opened to, and thereby constituted through, broader social, political and economic processes'. Hence, affect represents a power or a potential of the human body and human being; it is an expression of its 'vitality' and 'changeability' (Massumi, quoted by Shaviro 2010: 5). On the basis of this deployment of the term affect, Shaviro uses the expression 'aesthetic of affective mapping' to describe the building processes of affective maps which he understands, by reference to Jameson, Deleuze and Guattari, as 'tools for negotiating, and intervening in, social spaces' (Shaviro 2010: 6).

This same notion of affect as an expression of vitality and changeability intervenes in the analysis of the language and contents chosen by Roberto Saviano and his Staff in the complex work of social networking, namely the process of constant weaving of the network connecting the celebrity writer and his fans within the techno-magical environments of Facebook and Twitter.

If we observe Roberto Saviano's production on these two platforms, it comes out that until November 2011, the writer communicated by means of a narrative voice, which almost ever signed the posts or tweets using the name 'Staff', and almost ever referred to the writer only by his name 'Roberto'. The Facebook posts signed by the 'Staff' announced and promoted Saviano's public events; reminded the users the events previously advertised; and finally provided links to Saviano's articles, interviews and videos. For instance:

> 29/07/2011: 'Star and striped camorra: Obama's administration has ranked Campania's clans the second place of the criminal organizations threatening American economy'. Roberto Saviano's article on *La Repubblica* today. Staff.[10]

Since mid-November 2011, however, the year of social network usage boom on the part of celebrities (Spaziante 2016), something has changed in Saviano's online communication, as it is evident from the following posts:

> 18/11/2011: Dear friends, this page becomes always more a fundamental place for me to communicate with you all, directly and freely. By now we are so many, about a million and a half. Today, I'm writing to invite you to observe with great attention what is happening in New York against the financial drifting, thanks to the Occupy Wall Street Movement and its protest. So, please help me spreading the Saturday 19th November meeting at Zuccotti Park at 12 o'clock (6 p.m. in Italy). On that occasion I am speaking about how criminal organizations make profits from the crisis. A crisis denied for too long in our country. I'll wait for those of you who are in New York these days at Zuccotti Park. Those of you who won't be able to be there will receive real time updates on Facebook and Twitter. See you soon, Roberto Saviano.[11]
>
> 14/12/2011: I've read all your comments to my latest post. They are full of energy, empathy and ideas. For me, this is fuel. It's the square I can't go any longer, it's the place where I can meet the people I can't meet any more. We are almost one million and a half and we must start to make a thicker and denser network of activities of this place. . . . A hug, and thanks for your usual affection. Roberto.[12]

Therefore, in these words we can find Saviano's intentions concerning the use of the techno-magical platforms: a place for free and direct communication between the writer and his users, a space useful to the fans to receive real-time information, and finally a network to do more and more activities together. From that moment on, all Saviano's posts have been written in first person, and a higher and higher number of them has dealt with impressions, comments, opinions, recollections and also scraps of private life Saviano has decided to share with his Facebook and Twitter community. Nowadays, Saviano's online presence also includes statements of self-celebration (e.g. those referring to the increasing number of fans and followers of his social networks pages, or to the results of his latest works) and a plain gratitude and delight for this to a community he feels part of. Finally, he also never neglects to provide updates on his next public commitments and to endorse the projects he supports. The shift from the neutrality of the third-person narration and objectivity of the information conveyed to the first person and highly subjective involvement of the writer in his life on the social networks marks a radical change in Saviano's web communication. This can also be read as the sign of a change from the indirect representation of the writer as an old-style celebrity – who had to be constantly 'announced' on the scene by someone else and whose interventions had to be delimited in specific areas (books, articles, public events) – to the direct representation of a man's life, with virtues and faults. However, despite representing another step towards the desacralization of his 'heroic' public figure, this shift is perfectly in line with the construction of contemporary pop star identities (Spaziante 2016). Certainly, with this strategy Roberto Saviano manages to make the users even nearer to his persona: he *impresses* his web community *affecting* the fans, in the sense of touching them emotionally. The Italian equivalents of these verbs, impress and affect, are *impressionare* and *commuovere*, and perhaps it is not by chance that both verbs have a strong meaning relationship with the term 'affect', a key notion in this argumentation. As a matter of fact, *impressionare* is the Italian translation of the Latin verb *afficĕre*, from which the noun 'affect' derives, while the first meaning of the verb *commuovere*, according to the Treccani dictionary, is 'touching affects or feelings deeply'.

Recently, Roberto Saviano's communication on Facebook has undergone another change in terms of affective communication strategies: while in the past his use of this social network was mainly 'broadcast, vertical and one-directional' (Bonini 2012) – this means he never intervened with comments to his posts – nowadays his replies to users' comments are more likely to appear, although not so frequently. To say the truth, already in the past, by means of some sporadic references to what the fans wrote in their comments, Saviano seemed to read and observe very carefully the affective relationships that are 'vertically' (between the writer and his fans) and 'horizontally' built (among the fans) on his Facebook page, proving to be involved in them. This is particularly relevant not only because it reduces the fanatic fetishism of the celebrity, as I said before, but especially because the horizontal relationships might turn into the real agents of further relations, connections and exchanges giving birth to a fertile and participated communication. In its turn, this might emphasize the relationships among people and the desirable revolutionary potential I mentioned earlier.

To conclude, then, we should go back to Hardt and Negri's notions of 'multitude', the collective identities inhabiting the Empire, namely the 'new political subject' of the globalized age, and of the political as the 'beyond measure' where value takes place (356), the productive context is vital and the expression of labour is desire (357). Particularly, with regard to labour, the two scholars maintain that

> it appears simply as the *power to act*, which is at one singular and universal: singular insofar as labor has become the exclusive domain of the brain and body of the multitude; and universal insofar as the desire that the multitude expresses in the movement from the virtual to the possible is constantly constituted as a *common thing*. . . . The power to act is constituted by labor, intelligence, passion, and affect in one common place. (358)

Hence, this notion of labour is closely entangled with that of community, whose 'constituent power' is concretely constructed and configured by means of the common actions of labour, intelligence, passion and affect (358).

For Hardt and Negri, Empire exerts enormous powers of oppression and destruction, but the political task of the multitude inhabiting it is not simply that of resisting these processes, but to reorganize and redirect these processes towards new ends. Indeed, as they put it, the creative forces of multitude are able to build a 'counter-Empire', namely 'an alternative political organization of global flows and exchanges'. Hardt and Negri believe that 'the struggles to contest and subvert Empire, as well as those to construct a real alternative, will thus take place on the imperial terrain itself' and, in fact, it is just on this terrain that they have already begun to emerge: social media and digital platforms are only some of its manifestations. For Hardt and Negri, 'Through these struggles . . . the multitude will have to invent new democratic forms and a new constituent power that will one day take us through and beyond the Empire' (Hardt and Negri 2000: xv). In this theory by Hardt and Negri, which is based on a micropolitics of affect and on the valorization of the Spinozist 'power to act in terms of the singular and the common' (2000: 359), I think one can also grasp Castells's notion of utopias as material forms. Utopias, once again, involve the renewal of the current political, economic and social order thanks to a renewed power of the multitude and collective bodies inhabiting the beyond measure terrain. However, to make this happen, it is necessary to cultivate a vision and, as it is known, few people apart from intellectuals *can* do it and *have* the task to do it. Therefore perhaps it is not too pretentious to claim that the beginning of the path towards the greater awareness of Italian citizens leading them to the (virtual and real) square demonstrations of the last years began exactly with (or also thanks to) the huge alterdisciplinary event of *Gomorrah*. After all, fundamentally the whole of Roberto Saviano's interventions, disseminated all along new and old media, invited readers and audiences to pursue and defend strenuously their right to revolt, social justice, freedom of expression and above all their right to happiness.

FUTURE DIRECTIONS OF COMMITMENT

In the conclusions of this book, one of the questions structuring it recurs: who is Roberto Saviano? As we have seen, over the first ten years of his public career he has been defined in many ways: an engaged journalist, a great writer, an icon of anti-mafia campaigns, a pop star, a TV guest star, a radio storyteller, a cinema/theatre/TV series scriptwriter. Certainly, Saviano has been a huge media phenomenon, capable of dragging along millions of readers, spectators, listeners, followers and fans every time his presence has been announced in the media or in public events in squares, theatres, universities and bookshops. By means of his variegated experimentations and transmedia disseminations, Roberto Saviano strongly influenced the collective imaginary of the last years of Berlusconian Italy. His interventions have always been disrupting: they have posed questions, originated debates, provoked stances, thus proving that culture needs to be interpreted as a constant battlefield, where no once-for-all victories are obtained but always strategic positions to be won and lost, as Stuart Hall famously argued. Roberto Saviano's interventions have shown that thanks to literature and the different languages of cultural industry, it is *still* possible to build single and collective identities to be able to articulate agency, counter-power and counter-narration practices.

When he first appeared on the scene, some critics defined Saviano as another monstrous creature of Berlusconi's era, built *ad hoc* for media consumers by means of wise marketing strategies and a powerful brand. Yet, on almost every occasion over these ten years, he has been able to go beyond this accusation, proving to be capable of anticipating or interpreting the complex interrelations between local and global reality with great acumen, freedom from political conditionings and, yes, also an intelligent *branding*. It is not my task here to decree whether Roberto Saviano is a great writer, as this mostly depends on what one expects from literature. Nevertheless, like in *Gomorrah* (2006c), also in *Zero Zero Zero* (2013), in his latest novel *La paranza dei bambini* (2016) as well as in most of his articles and production, Roberto Saviano has always confirmed the importance of taking side, adhering to an understanding of literature, journalism and work in the cultural industry as practices of 'impegno', commitment, engagement. His idea of commitment, however, is completely different from what is generally meant in Italy. Indeed, the term 'impegno' is closely related with the period going from the end of the Second World War to the mid-1960s and with the ideology of Marxism, especially in Italy (Palumbo Mosca 2015: 1), considering mass culture as the new opium of the people or deliberate mystification (Morin 1962: 13). Instead, it seems that for Saviano the highest form of engagement is exactly 'transversity', that is the ability to speak to everyone, everywhere (even in shopping centres, as he has recently done), in order to exert leverage on reality and change it. Or, at least, attempting to change it. Roberto Saviano searches for wider and wider audiences, but he does not attack them, as they constitute his natural referent, to paraphrase Edward Said. For him, the problem is not mass society as a whole, but the group of 'experts' who mould the public opinion, making it conformist and subdued to supposed omniscient people exerting power (2014: 13). As a post-hegemonic intellectual, he encourages self-awareness and self-empowerment in all social strata as part of the construction of a bottom-up sub-politics defined by its constructive, critical attitude (Antonello and Mussnug 2009). This is definitely a renewed idea of engagement in our post-ideological age, an age resisting too restrictive definitions being mainly characterized by the pervasiveness of mass media and technologies of communication, the interdependence and hybridization of expressive genres and cultural products and horizontality in the construction of political and cultural dominants (Antonello 2012: 132). Indeed, as Antonello points out, whereas in the modern age literature found a central role in the cultural and intellectual education, in postmodern times the forms of 'impegno' must be found and created in a transmedia realm, made up of multiple discursive and expressive genres. Not only is the marginalization of literature an epochal change, but also the new prerogative of commitment. Political and civil engagement cannot be limited to high literature or highbrow literary genres like pamphlets, for instance. To encourage the emancipation of the audiences (readers, spectators, or web users) responding also to their changed tastes in terms of media consumption, engaged intellectuals need to confront themselves with the expressive genres of postmodernity, such as reportages, documentaries, non-fiction novels, graphic novels, blogs, TV series and even social networks. With regard to this, as I have tried to outline throughout the book, Roberto Saviano has reached absolutely outstanding results in terms of the quality of his 'products' and quantity of audience appreciation.

Whether Roberto Saviano's disruptive alterdisciplinary work has favoured the birth of new political and social discourses actually renewing the concepts of democracy, citizenship and civil engagement, and fostering people's empowerment in the life of Italy is definitely a matter of long-term evaluations. Nevertheless, Saviano certainly embodies a new model of intellectual, especially within the Italian context, still too reluctant and adverse to the figure of public intellectuals who are not afraid of using media as emancipatory means. But, the point is: will Roberto Saviano remain an 'event', a mostly solitary experience in the history of Italian cultural industry, or will the engaged intellectual class follow the transmedia direction traced by him? What will be the future of the Italian (and non-Italian) intellectual class? The answers to these questions, once again, have to do with the new dares of intellectual work in the post-ideological age. Now that intellectuals' distance from popular culture is evidently no longer a warranty for intellectual freedom, prestige and truthfulness, intellectuals should be more encouraged to meet the challenges of cultural industry. Despite they should always try to protect themselves from all forms of conditioning and obey only the ethics of research in the process of saying the truth to power and addressing the destinies of humankind, these challenges appear to be really urgent today, given the condition of the wider realm of intellectual labour (university, journalism, publishing, communication). Indeed, the vast majority of people working in these fields can be defined as 'intellettuali di se stessi' – a phrase roughly translatable as 'intellectuals of themselves' or 'self-intellectuals', hinting at the neoliberal refrain inviting everyone to become a self-motivated entrepreneur (Gentili and Nicoli 2015). They – but I'd better say we – are caught between the need to get 'visibility' and good 'reputation' investing their capital (human, cognitive, relational, economic) in forms of labour which are unpaid but 'measurable', and the sad awareness of fomenting a system based on subjection pratices worsening more and more the wage conditions of the intellectual labour itself. In this specific neoliberal context, public intellectuals may hopefully help solving this impasse by resisting the threat to elitism and conservatism which success may generate and, above all, building productive alliances and fruitful cooperation with the so-called self-intellectuals. Both categories of intellectual workers are expected to blend and strive together with a renewed class consciousness in order to pursue what should be their shared imperative of disrupting common sense, constantly reshaping and altering it within Italian culture and politics, two domains which are always in the process of becoming. What is at stake, for us all, is the enhancement of humanism.

NOTES

1. Alessandro Pecoraro has declared this intention during an online conversation with the author of this book.

2. Italian original: 'Ora so, grazie alle firme di migliaia di cittadini, . . . che qualcosa di mio è diventato qualcosa di nostro. E che paese non è più – dopo questa esperienza – un'entità geografica, ma che il mio paese è quell'insieme di donne e uomini che hanno deciso di resistere, di mutare e di partecipare, ciascuno facendo bene le cose che sa fare'.

3. Italian original: 'patto in cui l'emozione, gli affetti, e i simboli condivisi si pongono come le nuove matrici dell'essere insieme, come i nuovi presupposti di ogni fusione, confusione ed effusione collettiva'.

4. Born in 2002 outside Milan Justice Palace as a movement of civic resistance in defense of institutions and the judiciary system used by Berlusconi as a private matter, 'girotondi' actually expressed first and foremost a wide dissent of left-wing voters against the leaders of the centre-left coalition then named *Ulivo*.

One of the recognized leaders of this movement was filmmaker Nanni Moretti who unexpectedly, after a political assembly of *Ulivo* in Piazza Navona, Rome, in February 2002, pronounced from the podium an accusatory speech against the centre-left politicians. Moretti criticized them for being unable of self-criticism with regard to the political choices they made in the previous years; for being unable to catch the violence of Berlusconi's political and media strategies – for example, the emblematic servile journalism of Emilio Fede allowing Berlusconi to win votes for the elections – ; for being too moderate in facing Berlusconi's policies and, finally, unable 'to talk to the head, soul and heart of people'. 'With this kind of political ruling class – shouted Moretti from the podium – we will never win' (https://www.youtube.com/watch?v=8kuVgaPZyts).

5. The so-called *Rubygate* was the last sex scandal to emerge in Berlusconi's career as prime minister that caused him the charges of paying for sex with a minor, the seventeen-year-old Moroccan girl known as 'Ruby', and abuse of power to get her released by police after she was detained in another case.

6. They were Gustavo Zagrebelsky, Paul Ginsborg and Sandra Bonsanti. (Freedom and Justice, http://www.libertaegiustizia.it/chi-siamo/).

7. English version titled *Women bodies,* available at this link: https://www.youtube.com/watch?v=t4njg1Mu0gw.

8. This adjective derives from the verb 'to owl', *gufare*. Indeed, Matteo Renzi used the plural noun *gufi* (owls) to address the people who criticized his reforms. In his opinion, these people hoped his reforms would fail damaging the country.

9. Italian original: 'Renzi ha promesso molto ma alle parole non stanno seguendo i fatti e questo sta innescando un cortocircuito tra aspettative e realtà, deve capirlo. Che riformare il Paese sia impresa titanica ne sono consapevoli tutti. I problemi son così tanti e il consenso così necessario da mantenere che Renzi corre un grave rischio: invece di mutare il corso delle cose, gestisce il corso delle cose. Facendo piccoli, piccolissimi passi, rilevanti solo se paragonati al passato berlusconiano ma che non lo sono affatto se messi in relazione ai cambiamenti da fare'.

10. Italian original: 'Camorra a stelle e strisce. L'amministrazione Obama ha messo i clan campani al secondo posto tra le organizzazioni criminali che minacciano l'economia americana'. L'articolo di Roberto Saviano oggi su Repubblica. Lo Staff.

11. Italian original: 'Cari amici, questa pagina diventa sempre di più per me un luogo fondamentale attraverso cui poter comunicare liberamente e in maniera diretta con voi tutti. Ormai siamo tantissimi, quasi un milione e mezzo. Vi scrivo, oggi, per invitarvi a osservare con grande attenzione quello che accade a New York contro la deriva finanziaria, attraverso il movimento OccupyWallStreet e la sua protesta. Aiutatemi a diffondere, quindi, in queste ore l'appuntamento a Zuccotti Park di sabato 19 novembre alle ore 12,00 (ore 18,00 in Italia). Lì parlerò di come le organizzazioni criminali traggono vantaggio dalla crisi. Da una crisi troppo a lungo negata nel nostro Paese. Aspetto a Zuccotti Park chi in questi giorni sarà a New York. Chi non potrà esserci, verrà aggiornato in tempo reale tramite Facebook e Twitter. A presto. Roberto Saviano'.

12. Italian original: 'Ho letto tutti i vostri commenti al mio ultimo post. Ci trovo moltissima energia, empatia, idee. Per me divengono spesso carburante. È la piazza in cui non vado più, è il luogo dove posso incontrare chi non incontro.

Stiamo arrivando quasi a un milione e mezzo, e questo posto dobbiamo iniziare a renderlo una rete ancora più fitta e ancora più densa di attività. Ah, l'idea dei baffi, parrucca e naso di pongo per tornare a Napoli . . . mi attrae! Abbraccio e grazie per la vicinanza di sempre. Roberto'.

Bibliography

Adorno, T. W. and J. M. Bernstein (2011), *The Culture Industry. Selected Essays on Mass Culture,* London and New York: Routledge.

Allrath, G. and M. Gymnich (2005), *Narrative Strategies in Television Series,* London and New York: Palgrave Macmillan.

Amici, M. (2006), 'La narrazione come mitopoiesi secondo Wu Ming'. In *Bollettino di Italianistica. Rivista di critica, storia letteraria, filologia e linguistica,* 1.

Andò, R. and F. Comunello (2012), 'Vieni via con me. Consumo televisivo, social media e civic engagement'. In *Sociologia della Comunicazione,* 43: 89–104.

Antonello, P. (2012), *Dimenticare Pasolini. Intellettuali e impegno nell'Italia contemporanea,* Milan-Udine: Mimesis.

Antonello, P. and F. Mussnug, (eds), (2009), *Postmodern Impegno. Ethics and Commitment in Contemporary Italian Culture,* Bern: Peter Lang.

Arditi, B. (2012), 'Insurgencies Don't Have a Plan – They Are the Plan: Political Performatives and Vanishing Mediators in 2011'. In *Jomec Journal,* (1).

Attimonelli, C. (2010), 'Sigla Bondage, come ti lego e ti sospendo al video'. In *Eroi del quotidiano. Figure della serialità televisiva,* edited by F. La Rocca, A. Malagamba and V. Susca, Milano-Roma: Bevivino.

Attimonelli, C. and A. D'Ottavio, (eds), (2011), *To Be Continued. I destini del corpo nei serial televisivi,* Bari: Caratterimobili.

Attimonelli, C. and A. Giannone (2011), *Underground Zone. Dandy, Punk, Beautiful People,* Bari: Caratterimobili.

Baker, M. (1992), *In Other Words. A Coursebook on Translation,* London and New York: Routledge.

Barisione, M. (2009), *Comunicazione e società. Teorie, processi, pratiche del framing,* Bologna: Il Mulino.

Barthes, R. (1994), *Miti d'oggi,* Turin: Einaudi.

Bassi, S. (2015), 'Italy's Salman Rushdie: The Renarration of "Roberto Saviano" in English for the Post-9/11 Cultural Market'. In *Translation Studies,* 8 (1).

Benedetti, C. (2005), 'Genocidio culturale'. In *Nazione Indiana,* 18 January.

Benjamin, W. (1995), *Angelus Novus. Saggi e frammenti,* edited by R. Somi, Torino: Einaudi.

Bernardi, F. (2013), 'Roberto Saviano. A Media Phenomenon to Recount the South', in *New Perspectives in Italian Cultural Studies Vol. II,* edited by G. Parati, Fairleigh Dickinson University Press.

Bernardi, F. (2015), 'Italian Cultural Studies. Being on the Part of the Future'. In *Jomec Journal,* 8.

Berruto, G. (2010), *Prima Lezione di Sociolinguistica,* Roma-Bari: Laterza.

Bertoni, C. (2009), *Letteratura e giornalismo,* Roma: Carocci.

Boni, F. (2006), *Teorie dei media,* Bologna: Il Mulino.

Bonini, T. (2012), 'Appunti per un'anatomia della celebrità su Twitter'. In *Doppiozero,* 19 January.

Borràs Castanyer, L. (ed.), (2006), *Testualità elettroniche. Nuovi scenari per la letteratura,* Bari: B. A. Graphis.

Bowman, P. (2003), *Interrogating Cultural Studies: Theory, Politics and Practice,* London: Pluto.

Bowman, P. (2004), 'The Task of the Transgressor'. In *Culture Machine,* 6, https://www.culturemachine.net/index.php/cm/article/view/6/5.

Bowman, P. (2007), *Post-Marxism versus Cultural Studies: Politics, Theory and Intervention,* Edinburgh: Edinburgh University Press.

Bowman, P. (2008), *Deconstructing Popular Culture,* London: Palgrave Macmillan.

Bowman, P. (2010), *Theorizing Bruce Lee: Film – Fantasy – Fighting – Philosophy,* Amsterdam and New York: Rodopi.

Bowman, P. (2011), *Studi culturali. Teoria, intervento, cultura pop,* Bari: Progedit.

Bowman, P. (2012), *Culture and the Media,* Basingstoke, UK: Palgrave.

Brugnatelli, E. (2016), 'Gomorra prima di Gomorra'. In *Medium Italia,* https://medium.com/italia/roberto-saviano-gomorra-lettere-inedite-7412f0f87464#.ykfy7fuae, 17 June.

Brugnatelli, E. and C. Faggiolani (2016), *Gomorra: 10 anni di conversazioni su Anobii.* In *Le reti della lettura. Sulle tracce del social reading,* edited by C. Faggiolani and M. Vivarelli, Milan: Editrice Bibliografica.

Brunetti, B. and R. Derobertis, (eds), (2009), *L'invenzione del Sud. Migrazioni, condizioni postcoloniali, linguaggi letterari,* Bari: B. A. Graphis.

Brunetti, B. and R. Derobertis, (eds), (2014), *Identità, migrazioni e postcolonialismo in Italia. A partire da Edward Said,* Bari: Progedit.

Butler, J., E. Laclau and S. Žižek (2010), *Contingency, Hegemony, Universality. Contemporary Dialogues on the Left.* (Italian translation edited by L. Bazzicalupo, Roma-Bari: Laterza).

Calefato, P. (2000), *Lingua e discoso sociale,* Bari: Graphis.

Calefato, P. (2006), *Che nome sei*? Rome: Meltemi.

Calefato, P. (2008), *Sociosemiotica 2.0,* Bari: Graphis.

Calefato, P. (2009), *Gli Intramontabili. Mode, persone, oggetti che restano,* Rome: Meltemi.

Calefato, P. (2011), *Metamorfosi della scrittura. Dalla pagina al web,* Bari: Progedit.

Capovin, R. (2008), 'Beato quel popolo che non ha bisogno di intellettuali'. In *Ágalma* no. 15, Rome: Meltemi.

Cassano, F. (2009), *Tre modi di vedere il Sud,* Bologna: Società editrice il Mulino.

Castells, M. (2007), 'Communication, Power and Counter-Power in the Network Society'. In *International Journal of Communication*, 1: 238–266.

Castells, M. (2010), *The Rise of the Network Society* (2nd ed.), Hoboken, New Jersey: Wiley- Blackwell.

Castells, M. (2012), *Reti di indignazione e speranza. Movimenti sociali nell'era di Internet*, Milan: Università Bocconi Editore.

Cavaliere, F. (2010), '*Gomorrah*. Crime Goes Global, Language Stays Local'. In *European Journal of English Studies*, 14 (2): 173–188.

Chimenti, D. (2010), 'Il doppio binario del racconto storico in Gomorra di Roberto Saviano'. In *E/C Rivista dell'associazione italiana di studi semiotici*, 1–9; published online on 29 March 2010.

Chow, R. (1993), 'Where Have All the Natives Gone?' In *Writing Diaspora*, Bloomington: Indiana University Press, 27–54.

Chow, R. (2004), *Il Sogno di Butterfly. Costellazioni postcoloniali*, edited by P. Calefato, Rome: Meltemi.

Coretti, L. (2012), 'The Purple Movement. An Overview of Berlusconi's Italy through the Lenses of Social Movements'. In *Communication Management*, Spring Issue.

Cosenza, G. (2004), *Semiotica dei nuovi media*, Bari-Rome: Laterza.

Cosenza, G. (2010), 'Saviano, gli studenti e la violenza in piazza'. In *Disambiguando*, 20 December, http://giovannacosenza.wordpress.com/2010/12/20/saviano-gli-studenti-la-violenza-in-piazza/.

Cotroneo, R. (2004), 'Editori e media, i primi a voltare le spalle agli intellettuali'. In *l'Unità*, 19 February.

Dagostino, M. R. (2006), *Cito dunque creo*, Rome: Meltemi.

Dagostino, M. R. (2009), *Pubblicit@rte. Segni e visioni*, Bari: Progedit.

Dagostino, M. R. and P. Calefato (2007), *Il piacere del ritorno. Citazione, arti visive, comunicazione*, Bari: Progedit.

Dal Lago, A. (2010), *Eroi di carta*, Rome: Manifestolibri.

De Carlo, V. (2010), *Videosofia. Sentieri della filosofia attraverso la televisione intorno alla televisione*, Bari: Caratterimobili.

Derrida, J. (1989), *La disseminazione*, (Italian translation edited by S. Petrosino), Milan: Jaca Book.

Derrida, J. (1997), *Margini della filosofia*, (Italian translation edited by M. Iofrida), Turin: Einaudi.

Derrida, J. (2002), *La scrittura e la differenza*, (Italian translation edited by G. Vattimo), Turin: Einaudi.

Derrida, J. (2003), 'I Have a Taste for the Secret'. In *A Taste for the Secret*, edited by J. Derrida and M. Ferraris, Cambridge: Polity Press, 1–18.

Derrida, J. and B. Stieger (2002), *Echographies of Television*, Cambridge: Polity Press.

De Ruggieri, F. (2008), *I segni del cinema*, Bari: Progedit.

D'Orrico, A. (2011), 'Intervista a Roberto Saviano'. In *Io Scrivo. Corso di scrittura del Corriere della Sera in DVD*, Milan: Corriere della Sera.

Dyer, R. (2007), 'Stars'. In *Stardom and Celebrity: A Reader*, edited by S. Redmond and S. Holmes, London: Sage Publications.

During, S. (ed.), (1999), *The Cultural Studies Reader* (2nd ed.), London: Routledge.

Eco, U. (1964), *Apocalittici e integrati: comunicazioni di massa e teorie della cultura di massa*, Milan: Bompiani.

Eco, U. (1979), *Lector in fabula*, Milan: Bompiani.

Eco, U. (2010), 'Alfabeto per gli intellettuali disorganici'. In *La Repubblica*, 8 July.

Eco, U. and S. Hall (1985), 'Il ruolo degli intellettuali è quello di creare delle crisi'. In *Politiche del quotidiano. Culture, identità e senso comune*, edited by G. Leghissa, Milan: Il Saggiatore.

Fabbri, P. and G. Marrone (2000), *Semiotica in nuce (vol. I–II)*, Rome: Meltemi.

Fiske, J. (1989), *Reading the Popular*, London and New York: Routledge.

Fontanille, J. (2001), 'Lo schema passionale canonico'. In *Semiotica in nuce (Vol. II)*, edited by P. Fabbri and G. Marrone, Rome: Meltemi.

Forgacs, D. and R. Lumley (1996), *Italian Cultural Studies. An Introduction*, Oxford: Oxford University Press.

Gentili, D. and M. Nicoli (2015), *Aut Aut nr. 365, Intellettuali di se stessi. Lavoro intellettuale in epoca neoliberale*, Milan: Il Saggiatore.

Giannone, A. (2015), 'Bodies Rule! The Embodiment of Power between Fashion and Politics'. In *Jomec Journal*, 8.

Giovannelli, M. (2016), 'Sanghenapule tra mito e rito'. In *Doppiozero*, 6 April, http://www.doppiozero.com/materiali/sanghenapule-tra-mito-e-rito.

Gramsci, A. (1972), *Letteratura e vita nazionale*, Turin: Einaudi.

Gramsci, A. (1973), *Gli intellettuali e l'organizzazione della* cultura, Turin: Giulio Einaudi Editore.

Grasso, A. (2010), 'Vieni via con me. Un po' come a messa'. In *Corriere della Sera*, 24 November.

Gribaudi, G. (1996), 'Images of the South'. In *Italian Cultural Studies. An Introduction*, edited by D. Forgacs and R. Lumley, Oxford: Oxford University Press.

Grimes, W. (2007), 'Where Savage Parasites Rot a Nation from Within'. In *The New York Times*, 14 November.

Hall, S. (1994), 'Notes on Deconstructing the Popular'. In *Cultural Theory and Popular Culture: A Reader*, edited by J. Storey, London: Harvester Wheatsheaf.

Hall, S. (1997), 'Representation, Meaning and Language'. In *Representation: Cultural Representations and Signifying Practices*, edited by S. Hall, London: Sage Publications, 15–64.

Hall, S. (2001), 'Cultural Studies and Its Theoretical Legacies'. In *The Cultural Studies Reader*, edited by S. During, London and New York: Routledge, 97–109.

Hall, S. and D. Massey (2010), 'Interpreting the Crisis'. In *Soundings: A Journal of Politics and Culture* 44 (Spring): 57–71.

Hall, S. and M. Mellino (2007), *La cultura e il potere. Conversazione sui cultural studies*, Rome: Meltemi.

Haraway, D. (1991), 'A Cyborg Manifesto: Science, Technology, and Socialist-Feminism in the Late Twentieth Century'. In *Simians, Cyborgs and Women: The Reinvention of Nature*, edited by D. Haraway, New York: Routledge, 149–181.

Hardt, M. and T. Negri (2000), *Empire*, Cambridge, MA: Harvard University Press.

Janeczek, H. (2008), 'Siamo tutti Saviano?' In *Nazione Indiana*, 28 October.

Jenkins, H. (2006), *Convergence Culture. Where Old and New Media Collide*, New York: New York University Press.

Jensen, K. B. (1999), *Semiotica sociale dei media*, Rome: Meltemi.

Lamberti, E. (2000), *Marshall McLuhan*, Milan: Paravia Bruno Mondadori Editore.

Lombardi, A. (2016), 'L'esperienza di "Nazione Indiana" nella storia del web letterario italiano'. In *Le parole e le cose*, 30 May, http://www.leparoleelecose.it/?p=23193#_ftn33.

Lorusso, A. M. and P. Violi (2009), *Semiotica del testo giornalistico*, Rome-Bari: Laterza.

Lovink, G. (2006), *Zero Comments. Blogging and Critical Internet Culture*, New York: Routledge.

Luperini, R. (2004a), 'Il declino dell'intellettuale italiano'. In *l'Unità*, 18 February.

Luperini, R. (2004b), 'No, non ci sono più gli intellettuali di una volta'. In *l'Unità*, 11 April.

Luperini, R. (2007), 'La condizione degli intellettuali oggi', http://www.pasolini.net/saggistica_letteraturaRomanoLuperini.htm.

Marinelli, A. and G. Fatelli (2000), *Tele-visioni. L'audience come volontà e come rappresentazione*, Rome: Meltemi.

Marrone, G. (2001), *Corpi sociali. Processi comunicativi e semiotica del testo*, Turin: Einaudi.

Marrone, G. (2007), *Il discorso di marca. Modelli semiotici per il branding*, Rome-Bari: Laterza.

Marzocca, O. (ed.), (2004), *Moltiplicare Foucault vent'anni dopo*, Milan: Mimesis.

Massumi, B. (2002), *Parables for the Virtual*, Durham, NC: Duke University Press.

McLuhan, M. (2006), 'The Medium Is the Message'. In *Media and Cultural Studies: Keyworks*, edited by M. G. Durham and D. Kellner, Oxford: Blackwell Publishing.

McLuhan, M. and Q. Fiore (2011), *Il medium è il massaggio*, Mantua: Corraini Edizioni.

Morcellini, M. and P. De Nardis (1998), *Società e industria culturale in Italia*, Rome: Meltemi.

Morin, E. (1962), *L'industria culturale: saggio sulla cultura di massa*, Bologna: Il Mulino.

Morrione, R. (ed.), (2008), *Giornalismi&Mafie. Alla ricerca dell'informazione perduta*, Turin: Ega Editore.

Mottram, J. (2008), 'Gomorrah, Shot in the Name of the Godfathers'. In *The Times*, 9 October.

Palumbo Mosca, R. (2009), 'Prima e dopo Gomorra: non-fiction novel e impegno'. In *Postmodern Impegno. Ethics and Committment in Contemporary Italian Culture*, edited by P. Antonello and F. Mussgnug, Oxford: Peter Lang.

Palumbo Mosca, R. (2015), 'Fiction's Ethics'. In *Jomec Journal*, 8.

Pasolini, P. P. (2010), *Scritti corsari*, Milan: Garzanti.

Patella, G. (2008), 'Vita e morte dell'intellettuale postmoderno'. In *Ágalma* no. 15, Rome: Meltemi.

Ponzio, A. (1993), *Signs, Dialogue and Ideology*, Amsterdam and Philadelphia: John Benjamins Publishing Company.

Rancière, J. (1999), *Disagreement: Politics and Philosophy*, Minneapolis: University of Minnessota Press. Italian translation by B. Magni, (2007), Rome: Meltemi.

Ravveduto, M. (2007), *Napoli . . . serenata calibro 9. Storia e immagini della camorra tra cinema, sceneggiata e neomelodici*, Naples: Liguori Editore.

Rossi-Landi, F. (1972), *Semiotica e ideologia*, Milan: Bompiani.

Rossiter, N. (2006), *Organized Networks. Media Theory, Creative Labour, New Institutions*, Rotterdam: NAi Publishers.

Royle, N. (2003), *Jacques Derrida*, London-New York: Routledge.

Said, E. (1993), *Representations of an Intellectual*. In 'The Reith Lectures', *BBC Radio 4, June*, http://www.bbc.co.uk/programmes/p00gmx4c.

Said, E. (2014), *Dire la verità. Gli intellettuali e il potere*, Milan: Feltrinelli.

Saviano, R. (2005a), 'Scrivere sul fronte meridionale'. In *Nazione indiana*, 17 April.

Saviano, R. (2005b), 'Stampa di rispetto'. In *La voce della Campania*, 1 November.

Saviano, R. (2006a), 'E voi dove eravate?' In *L'Espresso*, 16 November.

Saviano, R. (2006b), 'Napoli. Dentro il vulcano'. In *Il terzo anello. Ad alta voce*, Radiotre, November.

Saviano, R. (2006c), *Gomorra. Viaggio nell'impero economico e nel sogno di dominio della camorra*, Milan: Mondadori.

Saviano, R. (2007), 'Intervista a Enzo Biagi'. In *Rotocalco Televisivo*, Raitre, April.

Saviano, R. (2008a), 'Codice Gomorra'. In *L'Espresso*, 19 February, http://espresso.repubblica.it/visioni/cultura/2008/02/19/news/codice-gomorra-1.7276.

Saviano, R. (2008b), 'O uccidi o sei servo'. In *L'Espresso*, 9 May.

Saviano, R. (2008c), 'Lettera alla mia terra'. In *La Repubblica*, 22 September.

Saviano, R. (2008d), 'Ogni voce che resiste mi rende meno solo'. In *La Repubblica*, 22 October.

Saviano, R. (2008e), *Gomorrah. A Personal Journey into the Violent International Empire of Naples' Organized Crime System,* New York: Picador.
Saviano, R. (2009a), 'Il coraggio dimenticato. Il valore degli africani e la speculazione delle mafie nel mondo'. In *La Repubblica,* 13 May.
Saviano, R. (2009b), 'Quando la verità è nelle parole dei lettori', Speech given at 'Scuola Normale Superiore' of Pisa, 15 May.
Saviano, R. (2009c), *La bellezza e l'inferno. Scritti 2004–2009,* Milan: Arnoldo Mondadori Editore.
Saviano, R. (2009d), *Beauty and the Inferno. Essays.* Translated from the Italian by Oonagh Stransky London: Verso.
Saviano, R. (2010a), *Gomorra. Viaggio nell'impero economico e nel sogno di dominio della camorra,* Milan: Piccola Biblioteca Oscar Mondadori.
Saviano, R. (2010b), *La parola contro la camorra,* Turin: Einaudi.
Saviano, R. (2010c), *Video-intervista a Current TV,* April.
Saviano, R. (2010d), 'Intervista a Gianpaolo Mazza'. In *Stilos,* June.
Saviano, R. (2010e), 'Lettera ai ragazzi del movimento'. In *La Repubblica,* 16 December.
Saviano, R. (2011a), 'Così si combatte il fango'. In *La Repubblica,* 12 April.
Saviano, R. (2011b), *Vieni via con me,* Milan: Feltrinelli.
Saviano, R. (2012), *Beauty and the Inferno,* London: Verso.
Saviano, R. (2013), *Zero Zero Zero,* Milan: Feltrinelli.
Saviano, R. (2014), 'L'Antitaliano'. In *L'Espresso,* 12 September.
Saviano, R. (2015a), 'Intervista a Chefuoritempo che fa'. In *Raitre,* 10 January.
Saviano, R. (2015b), 'Il giornalista licenziato su ordine del boss nella terra della camorra padrona in redazione'. In *La Repubblica,* 14 May.
Saviano, R. (2016), *La paranza dei bambini,* Milan: Feltrinelli.
Shaviro, S. (2010), *Post-Cinematic Affect,* London: Zero Books.
Sorice, M. (1998), *L'industria culturale in Italia,* Rome: Editori Riuniti.
Spaziante, L. (2016), 'Celebrità Pop: media, comunicazione, social media, identità', https://www.academia.edu/30252042/Celebrit%C3%A0_Pop_media_comunicazione_social_media_identit%C3%A0: 225–242.
Susca, V. (2010), *Gioia tragica. Le forme elementari della vita elettronica,* Milan: Lupetti.
Susca, V. (2011), 'La tecnica tra obsolescenza e reincanto'. In *TECNOSCIENZA. Italian Journal of Science & Technology Studies,* 2(1): 69–84.
Susca, V. and D. De Kerckhove (2008), *Transpolitica. Nuovi rapporti di potere e sapere,* Milan: Apogeo.
Tedeschi, E. (2003), *Vita da fan,* Rome: Meltemi.
Terranova, T. (2006), *Cultura Network. Per una micropolitica dell'informazione,* Rome: Manifestolibri.
Travers, B. (2016), 'Gomorrah' Review: Italian Drama Is a Darker, Grown-Up Version of 'The Sopranos', 24 August, http://www.indiewire.com/2016/08/gomorrah-review-season-1-tv-film-differences-sundancetv-1201719782/.

Trocino, A. (2011), *Popstar della cultura*, Rome: Fazi Editore.

Vattimo, G. (1989), *La società trasparente*, Milan: Garzanti.

Vito, M. (2010), 'A Narrative Discourse of the Twenty-First Century: The New Italian Epic'. *The Italianist* 30: 395–412.

Vito, M. (2011), 'Conversazione con Wu Ming 1 sul New Italian Epic e la critica letteraria italiana'. In *California Italian Studies*, 2(1), http://escholarship.org/uc/item/6nm5v9s1#page-72011.

Weber, M. (1968), *On Charisma and Institution Building*, edited by S. N. Eisenstadt, Chicago: University of Chicago Press.

Wu Ming, (2009), *New Italian Epic, Letteratura, sguardo obliquo, ritorno al futuro*, Turin: Einaudi.

Wu Ming 1, (2006), 'Wu Ming 1 su Gomorra', 21 June, http://www.robertosaviano.it/rassegna/wu-ming-1-su-gomorra/.

Wu Ming 1, (2008), *New Italian Epic versione 2.0. Memorandum 1993–2008: narrativa, sguardo obliquo, ritorno al futuro*, https://www.carmillaonline.com/2008/04/23/new-italian-epic/.

Wu Ming 1, (2010), 'Da lontano/ Da dentro. Note su nebulose, sguardi sovraccarichi e oggetti narrativi non identificati in letteratura e negli audiovisivi', *Limina, Rivista a cura del Programma dottorale PhD Planetary Collegium – M-Node*, 1, Milan: Nuova Accademia di Belle Arti.

Index

About the Author

Floriana Bernardi teaches English in Italian secondary schools. She has PhD in theory of language and sign practices from the University of Bari Aldo Moro (Italy). Her reseach interests encompass social semiotics, cultural studies, postcolonial and gender studies. In 2015–2016 she was visiting researcher associate at the School of Journalism, Media and Cultural Studies at Cardiff University (UK) where she guest edited an issue of *JOMEC* Journal devoted to Italian cultural studies.

www.ingramcontent.com/pod-product-compliance
Lightning Source LLC
LaVergne TN
LVHW101443200926
848483LV00001B/40